JOURNALING

Journaling

Catalyzing Spiritual Growth
Through Reflection

ADAM L. FELDMAN

MILLTOWN
publishing

Ellicott City, MD

"If you're interested in cultivating the spiritual discipline of noticing God, and journaling has been one such practice you've long considered important to introduce or improve within your spiritual journey, then the book you are holding in your hand is the gift you've long desired. Adam Feldman writes with a refreshing wit and a pastor's heart, with lots of practical helps for making journaling a highlight of your pilgrimage into a deeper walk with Jesus."

Stephen A. Macchia, Founder and President of Leadership Transformations, Inc., Director of the Pierce Center for Disciple-Building at Gordon-Conwell Theological Seminary, and author of several books including Becoming A Healthy Church *and* Crafting A Rule of Life

"I'm more excited about this book than I have been any book in a long time. Nothing has impacted my life like journaling. When I tell people they think it's a diary or they aren't writers—both have little to do with real journaling. Journaling is a spiritual discipline. I've defined it as 'a catalogue of reflections and a remembrance of events of what God is saying to you and doing.' I know of no better book than this. Stop thinking about being a writer or writing a diary—instead view it as listening and recording what God is saying to you. Thanks for writing this Adam, this is a HUGE overlooked need for serious followers of Jesus today."

Bob Roberts, Jr., Senior Pastor of Northwood Church and author of Bold as Love

"In this rich resource, Adam Feldman accomplishes his desire to encourage the faith of his readers and inspire them to practice the art and discipline of journaling. Along that way, he also effectively introduces readers to the broader world of contemplative reflection."

Randy Millwood, Team Strategist for Church Wellness of the Baptist Convention of Maryland/Delaware and author of To Love and To Cherish

"One of my favorite sayings about the spiritual life is, 'One person's piety is another person's poison.' For many, journaling has seemed more poisonous than pious! Often the poison has been the result of overly ardent journalers insisting that their way is the only way to pursue this spiritual discipline. Thankfully, Adam Feldman matches his passion for the benefits of journaling with flexibility and practicality in laying out a variety of approaches. Whether you are an experienced journaler, a tentative first-timer, or even someone who has 'written off' this practice as not for you, you will find Adam a helpful guide. As a church historian, I especially appreciated his reference to great journalers of the past, such as Augustine, Dorothy Day, and my personal favorite, Lancelot Andrewes."

Dr. David A. Currie, Director of the Doctor of Ministry Program and Associate Professor of Pastoral Theology, Gordon-Conwell Theological Seminary

Published by Milltown Publishing, P.O. Box 1258, Ellicott City, MD 21041. No part of this book may be reproduced without written permission from Milltown Publishing. www.milltownpublishing.com

ISBN-10: 0991220803

ISBN-13: 978-0-9912208-0-9

Cover design by Adrian Mathenia.

Cover artwork utilizes images from "Cutting and Holding the Feather," Johann Stäps, *Selbstlehrende Canzleymäßige Schreibe-Kunst*, Leipzig, 1784. This work is in the public domain in the United States because:

- it was first published outside the United States (and not published in the U.S. within 30 days) and

- it was first published before 1978 without complying with U.S. copyright formalities or after 1978 without copyright notice and

- it was in the public domain in its home country (Germany) on the URAA date (1996-01-01).

To all the fellow pilgrims and practitioners

who deign to pause long enough

to savor this fleeting life

along the Way

Home.

Thus says the LORD:

> "Stand by the roads, and look,
> and ask for the ancient paths,
> where the good way is; and walk in it,
> and find rest for your souls…"

– Jeremiah 6:16a-b

Contents

Acknowledgments

Thank you, dear reader, for sharing this journey with me by purchasing this book. I especially thank those of you who subscribe to my blog, who read it regularly, and who join in the conversation by offering comments. My two goals in writing this book, in keeping my blog, and in writing other works are to encourage spiritual pilgrims and to equip Christian practitioners. To this end, I pray that you are encouraged in your faith journey and equipped for ministry through reading this book!

I am indebted to the following people who gave of their time to read manuscripts of this book and offer critical feedback: Kim Feldman, Scott Feldman, Matthew and Monica Green, Michael Hoogeboom, Michael Roach, and Art Wong. The chapter titles, order and content of Chapter 5, stories of other journalers, and the second Appendix are largely the fruit of their input.

Thank you, Adrian Mathenia, for designing the book cover and Stephen Kilduff for your stellar copy editing.

Thank you, Stephen Macchia, for our lunch conversation at Gordon-Conwell Theological Seminary in May 2011. I mentioned to you that I wished to write this book and you looked me square in the eyes and said: "Write it!" Thank you for believing in me.

Thank you, Earl Gray, for being my coach and my friend. This book and my blog are results of our many pre-dawn conversations at Starbucks during the summer of 2012.

Thank you, Randy Millwood, for being a true spiritual friend and director. You are a trustworthy companion along the Way.

Thank you, Bean Hollow Coffee and Confections, for serving up the best coffee in the Baltimore/DC I-95 corridor. Every one of these chapters was typed at your tables.

Thank you, dear fellow Pastors of Metanoia Church. You are men who affirm God's work in my life and share the Way as authentic spiritual companions. Thank you, fellow Partners of Metanoia. You are wonderful fellow pilgrims along the Way, and I am blessed that you make it possible for me to serve you as Pastor of Spiritual Formation and Preaching. I could not have written this book without your support.

Most of all, I wish to thank my Lord and Savior, Jesus Christ, and my amazing wife, Kim. Without you two, I certainly could not have finished this book.

Kim, you make our home happy. Thank you for your sacrificial love for me, Abby, and Joshua. Thank you for believing in me and for sharing life as a true helpmate.

Jesus, you saved my life and redeemed my soul. Thank you for the gift of my family and spiritual community. This book is really all about you and for you. May it be a sweet offering of worship to you.

Introduction

Should You Journal?

I was talking with a good friend about this book recently. He knows that I am passionate about journaling and that I can be quite the journaling evangelist at times. In the midst of the conversation, he said something that I have heard time and time again. My friend said: "I know I should journal more often, but I probably won't."

Can you relate? Do you ever feel like you *should* journal?

Maybe you feel this way because a friend, pastor, or family member frequently shares with you how journaling has helped him or her grow spiritually. Maybe you feel this way because you paid the big bucks to get a really fancy journal and it is doing a great job collecting dust on your shelf.

Relax.

While I believe journaling is a powerful tool of reflection that can catalyze spiritual growth, I also know that journaling is not for everyone. God makes each of us unique in our personalities, life experiences, and even the means of our spiritual development. In other words, journaling may not be for you.

That said, you will not know for sure if you do not give journaling a good shot!

Maybe you have had a mixed record of starts and stops with journaling over the years. I am here to encourage you that it is not as daunting as you think. If you start off slow and steady, journaling can have a profound effect on your spiritual journey. Before you know it, you may even begin to identify yourself as a "journaler!"

Journaling a Journey

Journaling is by far one of my favorite spiritual disciplines. I have been journaling in one form or fashion since my mother gave me my first journal when I was about eight years old. Since then I have filled well over two-dozen journals.

My journals are a collection of poems, spiritual ruminations, daily experiences, sermon notes, feathers (yup), photos, drawings and sketches (admittedly poor quality), notes from my daughter, dried flowers and leaves, and quotes. Needless to say, my journals are a reflection of my life.

I have journals from my college years that contain entries from my first and last nights as a student.

On the night before I married Kim, I wrote a journal entry.

I journaled while riding on a train in the French countryside and also while sitting on a bench at Cambridge University.

There are crayon markings in one of my journals from when my daughter, Abby, got hold of it.

Some of my favorite photos are of Kim and I journaling in various coffee shops from Athens, Georgia, to Bar Harbor, Maine.

I love to journal, and I hope that you catch the bug, too! That is why I wrote this book.

About This Book

My primary desire in writing this book is to encourage your faith and inspire you to practice the art and discipline of journaling. Therefore, I suggest that you read this book all the way through and then return to specific chapters that address questions or thoughts you may have related to journaling. This is also why you will find each chapter a relatively short and manageable read.

You will quickly find that this book is about much more than journaling. This is because my second purpose is to introduce you to the world of contemplative reflection. For this reason, much of what you read in this book introduces you to some foundational ideas about spiritual growth (interchangeable with "spiritual formation") and reflection. It is upon this foundation that the great house of journaling is built.

There are many other wonderful resources out there that explore spiritual formation, reflection, and journaling. This frees me up to make this book a sort of "primer" or "introduction" to journaling and a contemplative, reflective life.

Here is how I structured the book for you:

- **Chapter 1: Awareness: The "Why" of Journaling** – This chapter contains a handful of reasons "why" you should keep a journal.

- **Chapter 2: Intentionality: The "What" of Journaling** – An exploration of "what" journaling is as a discipline of reflection and the role it serves in the faith journey of a disciple of Jesus Christ.

- **Chapter 3: Practice: The "How" of Journaling** – Simple tips on "how" to get started, or if you are already journaling, how to maximize the impact journaling can have on your spiritual development.

- **Chapter 4: Season: The "When" of Journaling** – More advanced tips on how to make the most of journaling by being sensitive to "when" things happen throughout the year and at various seasons of your life.

- **Chapter 5: Jesus: The "Who" of Journaling** – Guidance for working with Jesus to discern the spiritual fruit that He is producing in your life.

- **Chapter 6: Discipline: The "Where" of Journaling** – Tips on how to integrate journaling with other spiritual disciplines "where" journaling can enhance them. This chapter also explores how a journal helps you discern God's will.

- **Chapter 7: Reflection: The "Way" of Journaling** – Exploring how journaling and reflection fit into the broader context of life with God along His "Way."

- **Appendix 1: Setting Up a Moleskine Journal** – This details how I "set up" or prepare a new 240-page unlined, standard-sized Moleskine journal.

- **Appendix 2: Making a Plan to Journal** – This appendix brings together all of the practical advice that I give you into one place to help you make a plan to journal.

Here to Encourage

I sincerely hope this book encourages you in your faith journey and helps you fall in love with a spiritual discipline that has the potential to catalyze significant growth in your life. I want to hear from you about how you are exploring this discipline, so I give you my contact information at the conclusion of this book. Please stay in touch.

All right, let's get started!

Chapter 1

Awareness: The "Why" of Journaling

Half-Persons

Have you ever been in this situation? You are having a nice conversation with a friend over a cup of coffee when all of a sudden her phone pings. She pulls out her phone and, eyes on the phone, says to you: "Hold on a sec." She smiles—perhaps a chuckle, too—and then furiously pounds away at a text message. She smiles again, watches the phone send her message, puts the phone away, looks back at you, and says: "Sorry about that. So, what were you saying?"

My friend, you have encountered a "half-person."

I use the phrase "half-person" because that person is only half with you and half with someone else in that moment. Her body may still be with you, but her mind is engaged in conversation with someone else. Someone unseen. Someone interrupting your conversation. Possibly another half-person physically sitting with someone else.

We do not need scientific studies to tell us that texting while driving is dangerous. It is dangerous because a half-person is driving. There is an epidemic of half-persons driving cars, sitting in coffee shops, playing with kids at the playground, riding on subways, listening to lectures in class, eating dinner with family, bicycling to work, lifting weights in the gym, and sitting in worship services in houses of worship. Like zombies, they have the semblance of being present, but they are really not "all there."

Now, let's get real. Were you a half-person at some point this week or even today? I was. As I drove in to work this morning I pulled out my phone and called my wife, Kim, about something that I had forgotten to do. And as I currently revise this chapter while sitting in a coffee shop, my phone is on the table right next to my laptop. I have already checked email on my phone. Twice.

Journaling is a much-needed art and discipline in combating the root cause of the half-person epidemic in our society. That root cause is a deficiency of reflection. Your body can still function with a deficiency of vitamin D, but it is more susceptible to illness. Reflection is the vitamin D of your soul.

With this in mind, let's look at the broader umbrella that journaling falls under: the discipline of reflection.

Reflection in Scripture

Reflection is essential for the continued spiritual growth of the disciple of Jesus Christ. If we do not actively, intentionally, and regularly reflect on what the Lord is doing in our life, we often find ourselves discouraged, stagnant, or passionless in our faith. Journaling is one way we practice the art and discipline of reflection and cooperate with the Spirit to make sense of the deepening work He is doing in our soul.

While you will never find Jesus teaching about journaling nor a commandment to "journal" in the Bible, you will find God's people remembering the work of God in their lives and in their community. In fact, God even commands His people to remember Him and His Word. God's commands to remember are really commands to reflect on Him and on His activity in the world.

Perhaps the richest example of reflection is found in the festivals and holidays of the Jewish faith. These seasons of reflective worship serve as reminders of theological truths. For instance, Passover not only reminded the Israelites how God delivered them from slavery in Egypt, but also of His faithfulness to fulfill the promises made to their ancestor, Abraham. The Passover Seder, or "meal," still serves as a reminder of God's redemptive work.

It was during a Passover Seder that Jesus commanded His disciples—then and today—to engage in reflection on Him. Jesus used the Passover to institute what is commonly referred to as the Lord's Supper, Communion, or Holy

Eucharist. The Lord's Supper is a time for remembering Jesus' atoning sacrifice on the cross and His promised return. Christians today observe the Lord's Supper as a reflective discipline to examine their hearts and lives before God (see 1 Corinthians 11).

There are other forms of reflection in Scripture as well. In response to the Spirit's leading, Israel set up stones in various locations as a means of remembering the work of God in their community. One such experience is recorded in Joshua 4, when the people of Israel set up twelve memorial stones to mark the day they crossed the Jordan River into the land of Canaan. At another time, the people of Israel called upon the Lord to deliver them from the Philistines. To remember God's deliverance from their enemies, Samuel sets up a stone called "Ebenezer," which means "stone of help," to remind the Israelites of how God delivered them from their enemies (1 Samuel 7).

Persons in the Bible also frequently named cities, valleys, mountains, and other places to remember how God acted on their behalf. Abraham called the mountain where God provided a ram so that he would not sacrifice his son, Isaac, "The Lord Will Provide" (Genesis 22). The Israelites also named places to remember their sinful disobedience to God. In Exodus 17, Moses named the place where the people of Israel sinfully grumbled against God "Meribah" and "Massah," which mean "quarreling" and "testing."

The Bible itself is the definitive and authoritative reflective record of God's activity in our world. I am not saying that the Bible is a journal as we would understand a journal. However, it is a record of reflection—a revelation of God to His people past, present, and future. In other words, one purpose of the Bible is to remind us of God's redemptive activity in our world.

Along these lines, in *Spiritual Journaling*, Richard Peace says, "Taken together, the Old and New Testaments represent God's use of story to trace the thread of God's relationship with people down through the ages."[1] This is what you do when you journal. You are recording God's grand, epoch-spanning redemptive story as it unfolds in your limited, temporal sphere of existence here on earth. Your journal has the potential to record the continuation of the Holy Spirit's work in our world!

Now, your journal is not authoritative revelation like Scripture. Nonetheless, it does share one similar quality in that it recounts the real work and movement of God in the world. In fact, when coupled with reflection on Scripture, journaling helps us to conform our lives to God's revelation in the Bible—and not vice versa.

The Value of Reflection

The value of reflection to your spiritual growth cannot be overstated. Here are a few ways reflection influences your spiritual growth:

- **Discernment.** Reflection helps you to discern (not create) meaning in your actions and to discern (not create) God's will for your life.

- **Gratitude.** Reflection helps you to cultivate a deepening gratitude for the way Christ is at work in your life.

- **Awareness.** The ultimate fruit of reflection is a deepening awareness of Christ's *real* presence with you.

This is why I practice reflection through journaling: I want to discern God's will better, express gratitude for His grace, and cultivate awareness of Christ's presence with me.

Reflection in Contemporary Society

There are some counter-cultural reasons to practice reflection through journaling in our contemporary smart-phone, media-on-demand, always-connected society. One reason is because of the half-person epidemic. We are often so distracted by the "immediate" that we do not often take time to reflect on the "present." Journaling helps us to attend to our daily lives so that we become more "present" in each moment.

One reason why we are so distracted is that we have more opportunities available to us than most humans had historically. In *Spiritual Disciplines Handbook*, Adele Calhoun writes:

In a consumer society it's easy to accumulate experiences, believing the more we have the better! Yet experiences don't necessarily bring wisdom, nor do they automatically transform us. We need to listen and reflect on our experiences in the presence of the Holy Spirit to learn from them. Journaling is a way of paying attention to our lives—a way of knitting the vast ball of our experiences into something with shape that attests to the state of our souls.[2]

Do you resonate with Calhoun's assessment that accumulating experiences does not necessarily bring wisdom or transformation? Journaling helps us discern the "quality" of our experiences in the midst of the "quantity" of our experiences. Or, as Richard Peace writes, "Effective journaling begins by noticing the larger context of our lives."[3]

Both Calhoun and Peace use some very reflective words and phrases, like "listen," "reflect," "pay attention," "knit," "notice," and "the state of our souls." These words reflect a daily rhythm that is the antithesis of the half-person epidemic. A life lived in this rhythm is less prone to enslavement to technology, entertainment, and experience accumulation.

What Are the Benefits of Journaling?

Ask anyone who regularly journals and they will give you a list of ways they have personally benefitted from journaling. Of course, these lists are subjective and vary from person to person, so your experience may be somewhat different.

Here are some benefits that I have personally experienced by practicing reflection through journaling:

- **Making decisions.** Journaling helps me make significant decisions.

- **Discerning guidance.** Journaling reveals the subtle guidance of the Holy Spirit in my life over long periods of time.

- **Developing transparency.** Journaling provides a safe place for me to vent frustration, put words to thoughts, and to confess sin.

- **Deepening journey.** Journaling facilitates my focus in prayer and meditating on Scripture— especially in a home with small children!

- **Discovering legacy.** Because I penned my journey with the Lord, Journaling will someday inspire those I love after I have gone Home to be with Jesus.

Calhoun also offers a list of benefits to journaling:

- keeping company with Jesus through reflective journaling

- listening to God and praying your life

- slowing down and reflecting on where God shows up in ordinary routines

- remembering God's faithfulness throughout your journey

- leaving a legacy for others

- awareness of God's way of turning all things for the good of those who love Him (Romans 8:28)

- awareness of phases and stages of your personal pilgrimage[4]

These benefits that both Calhoun and I list above are, in large part, the result of reflecting on your journey with Christ. Journaling is just one of many disciplines of reflection and is also one of the most accessible reflective disciplines. In the next chapter, I explore "what" journaling is.

Awareness and Journaling: Nehemiah (approximately 445 BC)

More than any other book in the Bible, Nehemiah reads like a journal. From the first chapter through the beginning of the seventh chapter we are given significant insight into the interior world of Nehemiah's spiritual journey as he grieves over the broken state of Jerusalem, prays and fasts in search of God's will and intervention, mobilizes the Israelites to rebuild the wall of Jerusalem, and faces opposition to his leadership. The journaling-like style picks up again in chapter 13 when Nehemiah expresses his disappointment over the way his civic and religious reforms unraveled relatively quickly.

Nehemiah records prayers, writes about significant decisions, and details various other events. The book serves as a model for chronicling God's activity in the world. Chronicling God's activity in your journal nurtures awareness of God because your journal reveals the work of God in your life.

Reflection Through Journaling

Each chapter has a "Reflection Through Journaling" section at its conclusion so that you can use your journal to reflect on what you are reading. Answer the questions in these sections in your journal.

- Describe your pace of life. Is there space and time for reflection?

- Do you keep a journal? Why or why not?

- What has been your experience with keeping a journal?

- How do you sense yourself being drawn into the practice of journaling?

- What benefit or value of journaling mentioned above will impact your life today? Why?

Chapter 2

Intentionality: The "What" of Journaling

Dear Diary, er, um, Journal

What, exactly, *is* journaling?

For some people journaling is the same or at least similar to keeping a diary. When I think of the word "diary" I immediately begin hearing the theme song to the late 1980s/early 1990s TV show staring Neil Patrick Harris: *Doogie Howser, M.D.* (For those of you in my generation, you can thank me later for the "earworm" of the theme song playing in your head right now.)

The premise of *Doogie Howser* is that a brilliant teenager completes medical school and becomes a doctor. He is thrust out of the normal world of teenagers and forced to balance his professional career with his hormones. Every episode ends with Doogie sitting at his computer and typing up his daily experiences in a digital diary with a short "moral of the story" to sum up the episode.

For others, journaling is a lot like blogging. The word "blog" comes from a shortening of the word "weblog." I started blogging in 2003 and still keep a blog (www. adamlfeldman.com), but I do not use my blog as an online journal. It is more like a communal forum to engage other people in conversation. Blogs can also be kept "private," so a private blog may resemble a journal.

Journaling is at the same time similar and different from keeping a diary or blogging. Let's get a working definition of "what" journaling is.

Defining "Journaling"

Adele Calhoun offers a simple and helpful definition of journaling: "Journaling is a tool for reflecting on God's presence, guidance and nurture in daily comings and goings."[5] This gives us the "what" of journaling—it is a tool—and also the "why" of journaling—it is a tool for reflecting on God's presence, guidance, and nurture.

There are two things to note about Calhoun's definition. First, journaling is a tool for reflection. Journaling is not the only tool for reflection—it is one tool. There are many other tools for reflection in the spiritual journey, such as daily examen, spiritual direction, silence, solitude, and Sabbath.

Second, when practiced as a spiritual discipline, journaling deepens a believer's relationship with the Lord. According to Calhoun's definition above, three ways that the disciple's relationship with Jesus is deepened through journaling are:

- **Reflecting on God's presence.** Deepening awareness that God is with us every day.

- **Reflecting on God's guidance.** Deepening awareness that God is speaking to and with us every day.

- **Reflecting on God's nurture.** Deepening awareness that God daily provides for our every need, whether it be physical, emotional, spiritual, social, or mental.

Here is my current working definition: *Journaling is the disciplined activity of recording reflections on life for the purpose of facilitating a deepening daily awareness of Jesus' loving, personal, and active presence.* When I use the word "journaling" in this book, this is what I am referring to.

Journaling as a Spiritual Discipline

Journaling is a spiritual discipline. *Spiritual disciplines are activities (means) that we engage in (effort) by faith and with consistency (intentionality) for the purpose of making ourselves available to Jesus Christ and His transforming grace (end).*

Let's explore the four aspects of spiritual disciplines in my definition: means, effort, intentionality, and end.

Means

Spiritual disciplines are "means" for spiritual growth. They do not ensure spiritual growth as though there were some magical or scientific formula behind them. Rather, they are tools. As tools, spiritual disciplines must not be confused with the Person (Jesus Christ) and the power (His grace) behind spiritual growth. You need God's transformational grace in your life for your activity to be a spiritual discipline. On the other hand, all you need is good time-management skills and self-control for an activity to be self-help, a life-hack, or a great TED talk.

We see this reflected in John 5:39-40, where Jesus explains that Bible study is an important tool for spiritual vitality, but it must not be confused with the "Who" and the "how" of spiritual transformation. Jesus said: "You search the Scriptures because you think that in them you have eternal life; and it is they that bear witness about me, yet you refuse to come to me that you may have life" (English Standard Version).

It is possible to study your Bible every day and never encounter the God revealed in Scripture: Jesus Christ! Ultimately, the "Who" of spiritual growth is Jesus and not you. (More on this in Chapter 5.) Therefore, the "how" of spiritual growth is God's grace and not your effort. This is not to say that your effort does not matter. Applying effort through spiritual disciplines is the primary means for God's grace to transform you and grow you spiritually.

Here is an illustration from my own life. Several years ago, I slowly prayed through Psalm 119 over the course of a month. Psalm 119 is written in stanzas. Each stanza begins with the successive letters of the Hebrew alphabet and lauds the beauty, authority, and wisdom of Scripture.

I prayed my way through one stanza of Psalm 119 each day and journaled how God spoke to me through the Psalm. By the end of this spiritual exercise, I was transformed by the reality that God's Word, when meditated over, studied, and applied, reveals Christ on the pages of my Bible and also of my journal! Moreover, that Psalm has become a "friend" or "companion" along my spiritual journey. In other words, I experienced the truth of Jesus' words in John 5:39-40: studying Scripture is the means by which He revealed Himself and grew me spiritually.

Effort

"Let go and let God" is really an unhelpful phrase. Spiritual growth requires your effort in cooperation with God's grace. You do not put forth effort to earn God's favor—the Bible is consistently clear that God's favor is a grace freely given by God through faith in His Son Jesus Christ. However, without your effort, you will not grow in your faith.

Another way to say this is that your effort puts you in a place where God can, if He chooses, transform you by His grace. Just like a seed needs the right conditions for germination—good soil, water supply, and sunshine—the soul needs the right conditions—grace and effort—for transformation. For instance, with regard to Jesus' words in John 5:39-40 quoted above, without practicing the disciplines of Scripture reading and Bible study, it is impossible to grow spiritually.

2 Peter 1:3-11 is helpful in understanding the role of effort in your spiritual growth. I highlighted some phrases in this passage to help you understand the relationship between God's grace and your effort:

> *His divine power has granted to us all things that pertain to life and godliness,* through the knowledge of him who called us to his own glory and excellence, by which he has granted to us his precious and very great promises, so that through them you may become partakers of the divine nature, having escaped from the corruption that is in the world because of sinful desire. *For this very reason, make every effort to supplement your faith* with virtue, and virtue with knowledge, and knowledge with self-control, and self-control with steadfastness, and steadfastness with godliness, and godliness with brotherly affection, and brotherly affection with love. For if these qualities are yours and are increasing, they keep you from being ineffective or unfruitful in the knowledge of our Lord

Jesus Christ. For whoever lacks these qualities is so nearsighted that he is blind, having forgotten that he was cleansed from his former sins. *Therefore, brothers, be all the more diligent to confirm your calling and election, for if you practice these qualities you will never fall.* For in this way there will be richly provided for you an entrance into the eternal kingdom of our Lord and Savior Jesus Christ.

Let's unpack this passage in terms of God's empowering, transformational grace and your effort. First, God gives salvation and spiritual growth as a gift. It is "His divine power [that] has granted to us all things that pertain to [spiritual] life and [religious] godliness" (1:3-4). Thus, the effort you put forth in spiritual disciplines cannot earn God's favor because it is a free gift! No. Your effort is for something else, and that is the second thing.

It is precisely *because* you are given the free gift of salvation through God's grace in Jesus Christ that you must apply your effort to continue to grow spiritually. "For this very reason, make every effort...." (1:5). In other words, your car may be gassed up and the engine on, but until you apply effort to push down the accelerator pedal, you will not move an inch.

There are days when all I write in my journal is the date and the Scripture reference of what I read that day. Sometimes these days add up to a week or more. It never ceases to amaze me how there is a direct correlation between my effort applied in prayer, Scripture reading, and quality journaling and the relative fruitfulness of my relationship with Christ. This is not to say that these disciplines earn me some kind of "better" relationship with Christ. Rather, it is through my effort that I attend more closely to Christ in my daily life. My journal reflects this reality.

The third thing we observe in 2 Peter 1:3-11 is that through your effort and God's grace you *will* persevere in your faith. "Therefore, brothers, be all the more diligent to confirm your calling and election, for if you practice these qualities you will never fall" (1:10). If you are not experiencing a deepening intimacy with Christ or bearing the fruit of salvation, chances are you are either not trusting in God's empowering grace or not applying effort to cooperate with God in your growth.

Intentionality

Intentionality involves setting aside time and resources to engage in a spiritual discipline. Intentionality means engaging in an activity—any activity—with a purposed goal in mind (the "end" below). Otherwise, the activity is merely an academic, religious, or moralistic activity and, at best, a way to do-better-try-harder in hopes of improving the quality of your life. Intentionality to apply your effort in cooperation with God's grace in order to grow in your spiritual journey is what makes a spiritual discipline a "discipline."

Notice how the author of Hebrews weaves intentionality into the passage below:

> Therefore, since we are surrounded by so great a cloud of witnesses, let us also lay aside every weight, and sin which clings so closely, and let us run with endurance the race that is set before us, looking to Jesus, the founder and perfecter of our faith, who for the joy that was set before him endured the cross, despising the shame, and is seated at the right hand of the throne of God. – Hebrews 12:1–2

First, everything about Jesus' saving work is intentional. He *endured* the cross, He *despised* the shame, and He is *seated* at the right hand of God. These phrases indicate intentional action on Jesus' part—nothing about His death was accidental (see also Luke 9:51). It is because of Jesus' intentional work on your behalf that you are given all things needed for life and godliness (see 2 Peter 1:3-4).

Second, just as training for, running, and winning a race involves several intentional decisions, so does the race of faith. "Therefore...let us also lay aside every weight...and let us run with endurance." You are not competing against other disciples in a race as though spiritual growth were a competition. Rather, you are running for the sheer joy of running to, with, and for the founder and perfecter of your faith, Jesus Christ.

End

The "end," or desired "goal," is what makes journaling, prayer, Bible study, and a whole host of other activities spiritual disciplines. The end of all spiritual disciplines must be defined and understood according to what Scripture says about the goal of the Christian spiritual journey. Otherwise, disciplined activity is moving you toward someone or something else's goal.

According to the Bible, the goal of faith in Jesus Christ is nothing less than being formed in the image of Christ:

> And we know that for those who love God all things work together for good, for those who are called according to his purpose. For those whom he foreknew he also predestined to be conformed to the image of his Son, in order that he might be the firstborn among many brothers. – Romans 8:28–29

> And we all, with unveiled face, beholding the glory of the Lord, are being transformed into the same image from one degree of glory to another. For this comes from the Lord who is the Spirit. – 2 Corinthians 3:18

Being a better, more moral and righteous person is not the goal of faith in Christ. They are happy side effects as you cooperate with God and His empowering grace. But the goal of the Christian spiritual journey is to be radically transformed by God into the very real image of Jesus Christ. This does not mean that you become Christ or a deity like Christ. It means that you will love the Lord your God with all your heart, soul, mind, and strength, and your neighbor as yourself as Christ does (see Matthew 22:34-40).

In *Invitation to a Journey*, M. Robert Mulholland, Jr., explains that spiritual formation is a journey or a pilgrimage. He defines Christian spiritual formation as a process: "Spiritual formation is a process of being conformed to the image of Christ for the sake of others."[6] Notice how his definition of spiritual formation, or "spiritual growth," is "for the sake of others." This means that, as amazing as the transformation is that God works into your life, the reality is that through your spiritual transformation, God encourages other believers and evangelizes the lost.

As a pastor, I have counseled quite a few believers who were discouraged in their faith because they could not achieve a spiritual goal that is not consistent with what the Bible says is the end goal of spiritual formation. For some, it was being absolutely free from giving in to lustful activities; for others, it involved no longer flying off the handle with anger. Certainly the cessation of lustful and angry behaviors is part of being formed in the image of Christ, but the goal of spiritual growth cannot possibly be reduced to only being free from these behaviors. In this case, the goal of spiritual formation is a behavioral target and not a life-long, all-encompassing, all-inspiring goal of being formed in the very image of Christ.

Journaling and Other Spiritual Disciplines

Now that you have an understanding of what spiritual disciplines are and what I mean by "journaling," let's briefly look at how journaling can enhance other spiritual disciplines. While I explore this thought at length in Chapter 6, here are a few ways that I have personally experienced journaling enhancing other spiritual disciplines:

- **Fasting.** Every time that I fast I experience different physical sensations, spiritual battles, and fresh insights into Scripture. Journaling while fasting has helped me grow in the discipline of fasting by recording all of this.

- **Meditation.** In meditation, I ruminate and ponder over brief passages of Scripture or individual verses. Journaling what the Spirit reveals to me in these times helps me remember, obey, and act. Over the years I have recorded several verses in my journals that I have meditated on.

- **Prayer.** Do you have trouble concentrating while praying? I do, too. Internal and external noises often distract me while praying. Sometimes I write my prayers out to Jesus in my journal. This provides an amazing record of answered and redirected prayers.

- **Solitude.** My journals are with me during every time of extended solitude. These one to three nights alone with the Lord are precious, and I have a record of them that helps me track my journey with the Lord.

- **Bible study.** I write down what I am learning in my times of concentrated Bible study. Recently I journaled my way through all four Gospels. Over the years I have journaled through much of the Bible.

- **Worship.** While on a recent prayer retreat with our church, I found myself in a field full of wildflowers and birds. I was reminded of Jesus' words in Matthew 6:25-34 that Father cares for the flowers and the birds, and cares even more for me. I worshipped Jesus for His care and faithfulness. As an act of reflection, I dried one of those wildflowers and pasted it into my journal.

"Being" always precedes "doing" in the spiritual journey. As you read above, it is because you have received the free gift of salvation in Christ—"being"—that you now must engage in spiritual disciplines—"doing"—to grow in that salvation. This is why I tackled the "being" aspects of journaling first: the "why" and the "what."

In the next chapter, I tackle the "doing" of journaling.

Intentionality and Journaling: Jonathan Edwards (AD 1703-1758)

Jonathan Edwards was a prominent Reformed preacher and theologian who played a critical role in the First Great Awakening (1730s and 1740s) in the United States of America. Edwards was a prolific writer, producing countless sermons and treatises. We are fortunate to have the vast majority of his works still available in publication today.

One of Edwards' more well known works is his *Resolutions*. Edwards kept this list of seventy resolutions in a journal and read over them weekly. They guided his personal spiritual journey and helped him to live intentionally according to the convictions that the Lord laid upon his heart. His *Resolutions* serve as an example of how a journal aids in bringing intentionality to our spiritual journey and ministry.

Reflection Through Journaling

- What spiritual disciplines have helped you grow in the image of Christ?

- What are some of the benefits that you have experienced reflecting on your spiritual journey?

- Other than journaling, what other methods or tools for reflection are you aware of?

- In what way will journaling enhance your prayer or Scripture reading in the coming days?

Chapter 3

Practice: The "How" of Journaling

Right or Wrong?

Relax. There is no "right" or "wrong" way to keep a journal.

When it comes to "how" to keep a journal, I have found that there tend to be two primary camps. On one side are proponents of rigorously detailed systems. On the other side are advocates of casual, informal writing. And, of course, there is everything in between.

Your personality type, life experiences, time constraints, and many other factors will affect where you fall on the spectrum of how to keep a journal. What is most important is that you write in your journal on a consistent basis. Consistency is an aspect of intentionality. As I explained in the previous chapter, intentionality is a key element to what makes journaling a spiritual discipline.

What does consistency look like for you? Can you write daily? Should you write a couple of times each week? What about writing once a week during your weekly Sabbath? How about writing during intense seasons of pain or joy? All of these are legitimate options for how to journal consistently.

With this in mind, what you read below are five tips on how to keep a journal. Feel free to adapt what you read in any way that you wish to suit your journaling preferences.

Tip 1: Get a Journal

You need to get a journal if you are going to practice the art and discipline of journaling. (I know. I am one for the obvious, right?) The good news is that there are many, many options out there, and some are as cheap as free!

Small Journals

I encourage folks who are new to journaling or are returning to journaling after a few frustrating starts to purchase a small journal. By "small" I mean 100 pages or less and physically smaller than a more standard-sized journal. Moleskine makes some great mini-journals in both soft and hard covers.

The reason why I suggest that you start (or restart) with a small journal is because you will fill it up faster than a larger journal. There is an existential high-five that you experience when you finish writing on that last page, and it will motivate you to continue practicing the art of journaling.

Standard-Sized Journals

After you successfully fill a small journal, purchase a more standard-sized, archival (meaning "acid-free") journal. These do not have to be expensive. For many years I used acid-free artist sketchbooks that I found at Barnes & Noble for under $5. I have since moved on to standard-sized unlined Moleskine journals.

Inexpensive vs. Expensive

Since we are on the topic of cost, let me reiterate that you do not need to break the bank to get a good journal. If you are just starting out (or restarting) journaling, I suggest that you do not purchase anything fancy or expensive such as the Moleskine journals that I use. (The average cost of the journal I use is around $18). A spiral notepad or an inexpensive acid-free artist's sketchbook will do just fine. Work within your budget.

Lined vs. Unlined

My personal preference is to use journals without lines. I choose unlined journals because I like to draw and occasionally write on both pages when I am planning a project or sketching out a sermon. Whether or not you use lined or unlined journals, choose within your preferences. Remember, your journal is *your* journal—not mine or anyone else's.

Digital Journals

Chances are that you have a blog or you have had a blog in the past, since there are a gazillion out there. Blogs are great ways to keep digital journals, since there are both free and paid options. Additionally, you can blog from any mobile, notebook, or desktop device with internet access. You can make your blog private, share it with specific people, or make it public. You can even keep a public blog on Facebook.

If you are of the digital ilk, skip the paper journal and go straight to a blogging platform. I have personally blogged on WordPress, Blogger, and Typepad platforms over the years and recommend any of them to anyone interested in blogging or digital journaling. There are free versions to these platforms, they are very user-friendly, and they are easy to set up.

Blogging platforms are just one of many ways you can keep a digital journal. There are new apps for tablets and smartphones coming out every week. You could also choose to use Google Drive, Evernote, or any number of other cloud-based services to keep journal entries, since these services sync via the cloud with multiple devices.

Tip 2: Write Your Life

Whenever I teach on the discipline of journaling, inevitably I get asked a question that goes something like this: "Should I just write about my 'spiritual' activities—Bible study, prayers, sermon notes, devotionals, etc.—in one journal and keep a separate journal for my 'daily life?'"

I understand where this question comes from, because years ago I kept at least three journals: one for my "spiritual" activities, one for my "daily life," and one for my poetry.

Shortly after I graduated from college, I transitioned to one journal that integrates everything. This decision came from a deep conviction that there is no real distinction between "secular" (i.e. "daily life") and "sacred" (i.e. "spiritual" activities) for the disciple living *in Christ*.

This is not the same thing as saying that there are no "sinful" or "fleshly" aspects of my life that grieve God. Rather, it is to say that whether or not I am aware of it, God is with me as I change diapers, commute to work, read my Bible, go for a jog, mow the lawn, pray for my family, and watch my favorite sports team on TV.

In Colossians 3:1-4, Paul explains that for a disciple, Christ *is* your life (see 3:4). He goes on to implore the Colossians to put to death those things that grieve God (3:5-11). Things like covetousness, idolatry, and lying. Then, he flips the argument and implores the Colossians to put on the things of God (3:12-17). Things like humility, patience, and meekness. It seems to me that we should look to lists such as these to identify what grieves the heart of God and use Biblical words like "sinfulness" and "sins" to describe them.

Paul concludes his argument with these great words in 3:17: "And whatever you do, in word or deed, do everything in the name of the Lord Jesus, giving thanks to God the Father through him." This is a great reminder that for the disciple of Jesus Christ, *everything* we do is in company with God. That means our sins and our virtues. Everything is done in company with God. Some things you do grieve God's heart, and others look a whole lot like Jesus. Thus, I believe that any distinction between the "secular" and "sacred" things of life is pretty subjective. (I explore this idea more in Chapter 5.)

On a personal note, keeping one journal deepened my awareness of God at work in everything that I do and everywhere that I go. When I record what I used to consider as "spiritual"—like prayer concerns and thoughts on Scripture—as well as what I used to consider "mundane"— like what I did that day, my hopes and dreams, lists of things I need to do, and what is frustrating me—I find Christ moving in and out of my daily rhythm. I am not there yet, but slowly the mundane is becoming less mundane and the "secular" is quite "sacred."

Tip 3: Develop Your Style

As with all spiritual disciplines or any worthwhile activity, the best way to journal is to *just do it*. Just write. Over time you will begin to learn what does and does not work for you, and this is how you will organically develop your own journaling style.

Here are two important things to keep in mind as you develop your style of journaling:

Figure Out What Suits You

I used lined journals through college and then transitioned to unlined artist sketchbooks and journals since, because I like to draw from time to time. I also stopped using spiral-bound journals after college because they get messed up in my backpack.

As I mentioned above, my favorite brand of journal is Moleskine. There are many different kinds of Moleskine journals, such as lined, unlined, graphing paper, large, small, and even travel journals with subway maps of major cities.

One great advantage of Moleskine journals is that they have a pocket in the back. I use the pocket in my journal to keep photos of my wife, Kim, and my children, Abby and Joshua. I also keep a few business cards, and a sheet with the names of all the members in our church so that I can pray for them. I am such a huge fan of Moleskine that I wrote an appendix to this book describing how I set up my Moleskine journals. (Oh, and, in case you are wondering: I do not get any kickbacks from Moleskine for lauding their stellar products. I am just a fan!)

Use Your Voice

Do not try to be the world's best writer. Just be honest, authentic, and write for two people only: Jesus and yourself. Besides, you will find more joy writing if you can just be open and honest in your language. Adele Calhoun says that journaling "is a way for you to be with God and your thoughts, not an exercise in language arts."[7] This is not an open-book test and you will not be graded, so be yourself!

Tip 4: Develop Your System

I briefly touched on my journaling system—the way I go about journaling—in the second tip above. My system is admittedly informal with regard to what I write, and a bit more formal in how I set up my journal (see Appendix 1). This may not work for you, since you may prefer to have a more systematic approach to your journaling. Your system not only includes how you organize your journal, but also the physical environment in which you choose to journal.

Organization

If you desire a more systematic approach, I suggest that you study the system that Richard Peace advocates in *Spiritual Journaling*. As you read what he has written below, notice how he distinguishes between a "journal" and a "diary." Remember, it is intentionality that transforms journal keeping into a spiritual discipline instead of a diary of your daily life:

> A journal is not just a diary in which you record each day's impressions. In a journal you record a variety of impressions, written from different vantage points and in different ways, with one section feeding into the other sections. Thus, to maximize the value of the journal, it helps to divide it into sections. The following divisions are suggested:
>
> *Daily:* staying in touch with your life as it unfolds
>
> *History:* reconstructing the contours of your past
>
> *Dialogue:* journaling a "conversation"
>
> *Pilgrimage:* exercises to promote personal growth

Bible study: analyzing and applying Scripture

Dreams: recording your nightly images

Musings: recording insights, thoughts, and reflections

Family: marking key events in your family's development

Work: keeping notes and materials related to your job[8]

I cannot speak for you, but the idea of keeping a journal with nine or more sections seems a bit overwhelming. It reminds me of the very reasons why I opted to keep only one journal instead of multiple journals. To his credit, Peace suggests including all of these sections in one loose-leaf binder with dividers, which implies a measure of integration. In other words, although he advocates for multiple sections in one journal, they all feed "into the other sections" so that you get a comprehensive picture of your life. If this appeals to you, by all means, pick up Peace's book and go deeper!

Environment

Whatever system you choose—whether informal or systematic—the environment where you journal matters. Find a place to write that is:

- **Comfortable.** If at all possible, you should be physically comfortable and relaxed when you journal. Pay attention to the kind of chair you choose to sit in, the height of the table before you, the temperature in the room, the weather (if you are journaling outside), and even the smells in the room.

- **Quiet.** The least amount of distraction, the better.

- **Ambient.** A reasonable alternative to "quiet" is ambient noise, like the sonorous murmur of conversations in a coffee shop.

- **Private.** Find a place where you will not feel like people are looking over your shoulder while you write.

Tip 5: Make the Time

"But, I don't have time to journal!" My response to this complaint is simply: "Really? I don't believe you."

Make a Plan

As with exploring any spiritual discipline new to you, begin journaling by starting small and consistent in order to avoid discouragement. Often, people think they need to journal every day and write for an arbitrary amount of time or number of pages. However, journaling for 10-15 minutes two to three times a week for six weeks is a solid start. At the conclusion of six weeks, you will find that journaling has become part of your weekly rhythm and it may actually be more difficult to *stop* than it was to *start*.

Redeem Time

If you write for, say, 15 minutes twice a week, you can easily fill a small journal in less than a year. That is 30 minutes each week, or an average of just over 4 minutes a day. Would you be willing to give up a 30-minute TV show or to wake up a few minutes earlier a couple times each week if it could potentially have a lasting, transformational impact on your spiritual growth? Redeem the time allotted you by God with reflection.

A Note to Parents

A quick note to moms and dads of young children. You are probably thinking: "You come over to my house for a day and help me scrape dried snot off the armchair, fish the hair barrette out of the air vent, clean up the explosion of spilled milk from the floor, sofa, and wall, and THEN tell me that I have time to journal!" (Circumstances in this example may or may not have been what I had to do earlier this week in a 10-minute period of time.)

As a parent of two small children and the husband of a wife who stays home most of the week to care for them, I certainly understand the unique time constraints and circus-like balancing act of navigating schedules and life in general. Do not give up on me, yet! I address specific ways parents can find time for journaling in the next chapter. In the meantime, I still stand by my conviction that you do have time to journal. (Okay, spoiler alert for next chapter: one way you can make time is by asking your spouse to give you a few minutes a couple of times each week to journal.)

Bonus Tip 6: A Good Pen

Those are my five tips on "how" to keep a journal. Here is a bonus tip for those of you who, like me, prefer paper to digital. Just as we started our discussion on how to keep a journal with the obvious—"get a journal"—we will end with the obvious. *Get a good pen.*

(For those of you who prefer journaling digitally or with a pencil, you can pretty much disregard this bonus tip. I know. You feel cheated. Go ahead and journal your feelings.)

Here are some suggestions for choosing your pen (don't worry—I do not get any kickbacks from the pen companies mentioned below):

- **Smudge-free.** Choose a pen that will not smudge much. Most packaging for pens will indicate the size of the pen tip. Anything over a 0.5-mm ball is in smudge-territory. Smudging is one reason why some people prefer to journal with pencil.

- **Click or no-click?** If you are like me and you carry pens in your pocket, go "no-click." There is less chance of the pen opening in your pocket and ruining your favorite pair of pants. This is why

I use pens with caps. If you do not keep pens in your pocket or use a pocket protector, go for a good clicking pen like the Pentel EnerGel needle tip 0.5-mm pen.

- **What is your budget?** Find a pen within your budget. While gel ink looks better on paper than ballpoint ink, you do not have to spend a lot of money to get a good gel ink pen.

- **What color?** Determine what color you want to write in your journal. Kim uses blue pens to write in her journals. I use black to write in mine. If either of us forgets our pen when we have a coffee shop journaling date, you will know because our journal entry changes color for that day.

I use capped Pilot P-500 extra fine 0.5-mm pens. There is as much chance of you finding them in a store as there is for the Chicago Cubs to win the World Series, but you can find them online. I buy them in bulk from Amazon. Who knows? If enough of us start buying these pens online and this thing goes viral, we may find the elusive Pilot P-500 in stores again!

Reflection Through Journaling

The focus of this chapter is a bit different from the other six chapters in this book. It focused more on the nuts and bolts aspects of journaling than any other chapter in this book. Thus, in lieu of offering you a snapshot of another journaler, I give you Appendices 1 and 2, which describe how I set up my journal and help to you set up your own.

In addition to the two Appendices, the following reflection questions will help you practice journaling:

- What is keeping you from journaling today or tomorrow? Why not make time and make it happen?

- What one thing will you do in the coming days to begin journaling?

- What additional tips would you add to this list? Please go to the *Journaling* page on my blog and offer comments to help others along the journey.

Chapter 4

Season: The "When" of Journaling

Seasons of Life

When I was in college, I journaled at the library, on the grassy campus lawns, at the local coffee shop, and late at night after play rehearsals. When I was in seminary, I found time to journal in the mornings over coffee in my apartment and in the evenings over coffee again at the coffee shop. Before we had children, Kim and I loved to journal together at the coffee shop. Now that we have children, our journaling habits look very different.

Whether you are a child who cannot wait for summer break, a teenager who cannot wait to graduate high school, a college student who can barely see the light at the end of the tunnel to finish your degree, a single adult who desires to be married, a single-again adult who is healing from wounds and putting the pieces of life together again, a married-without-kids couple, a married-with-kids couple, a single-with-kids mom or dad, or an empty nester, your current season of life has not escaped the sovereign hand of God.

Let this truth encourage you: God knows what your today is like because He was "here" today when you were "there" yesterday. This means that our Creator wants to meet you right here and right now!

Three Life Suckers

As a pastor, I periodically encounter frustrated young parents (like myself) who lament over the loss of the "good old days" when they had time to journal, pray for long periods of time, go to Bible studies, stay up late at social events, or spend half a day in a coffee shop. Unfortunately, such an attitude betrays a deep-seated discontentment with the current season of life that God lovingly and sovereignly placed you in *today*.

Your current season of life is the "when" of your journaling. Discontentment with your current season of life manifests itself in ways that suck the joy, peace, contentment, love, and fruitfulness out of your life today. If you are not careful, these "life suckers" will detrimentally affect your love for God and for others.

The following are three life suckers that, if you are not careful, will make the otherwise fertile soil of your current season of life fallow ground.

Life Sucker 1: Entitlement

Entitlement manifests in many ways. You believe you are entitled to more money, more respect, more fame, more fulfillment, more time, more silence, less distraction, and less noise. I could go on and on creating a list of entitlements, but I think you get the idea.

When entitlement takes root in a parent, he begins to blame his children (gifts from God) and God (THE supreme gift) for his perceived "lack of time." When entitlement takes root in a single adult, she begins to blame her singleness (a gift from God) and God (THE supreme gift) for her "lack of fulfillment." Entitlement robs you of joy because you spend significant energy blaming yourself, others, or God for what is less than desirable about your current season of life.

Are you wrestling with entitlement right now? Here is a simple test: Do you blame God for what you do not have ("your" spouse, job, house, children, etc.) as though He promised these things to you?

Here is another test: What are you seeking that until you possess it you cannot be completely fulfilled?

Paul speaks about the seasons of singleness and marriage in his first letter to the Church in Corinth.

Only let each person lead the life that the
Lord has assigned to him, and to which
God has called him. This is my rule in all
the churches.... So, brothers, in whatever
condition each was called, there let him
remain with God. – 1 Corinthians 7:17, 24

Contentment is first embraced by acknowledging God's sovereign and good rule in your life (His "providence") and believing that He has "assigned" you this season of life for right now. The next step is to root out those areas of entitlement unique to your own temptations and longings. This is where journaling can help you organize your thoughts and understand your longings.

Kim and I moved to the Ellicott City, Maryland, area in the summer of 2005 to start Metanoia Church. Our planting team of five persons—ourselves included—opted to pursue an intentionally organic growth model. This had implications for how we went about our mission. For instance, we have never advertised our church. Additionally, we have never conducted a large evangelistic event. Instead, we have relied solely on being known via word-of-mouth, and we have partnered with our city to facilitate the annual civic festivals and events in our town.

The flip side of our decision to grow in an intentionally deep and relational way is that Metanoia grew relatively slowly compared to some other church starts. Early on we doubled in size annually for a few years. Sounds great, right? Well, remember: *we started with five people.*

About three years into planting Metanoia, I faced a crisis. Metanoia was not growing at the pace that I had hoped it would. *Not even close.* I got so frustrated and depressed that I actually considered throwing in the towel.

Rather than throwing in the towel, I stepped back and began journaling my thoughts and feelings. There on the pages of my journal in 2007, I saw clear as day that I had a deep root of entitlement. I was frustrated and depressed because I felt entitled to rapid growth and also to being the next great well-known church planter.

Another thing that I noticed on those pages is that Metanoia was growing exactly the way we planned her to grow: deep and organically. As I reviewed my 2005-2007 journals, I began to realize that our strategy was actually working the way it was designed to work. This meant relatively slow growth compared to some other new churches, but it also meant consistent growth in life transformation.

Metanoia is now in our ninth year of mission and ministry, and we are still experiencing God transforming lives along with consistent numerical growth.

My friend, you must deal with entitlement because it can metastasize into something worse.

Life Sucker 2: Bitterness

When entitlement deepens its roots in your heart, it grows into a nasty, suffocating vine of bitterness. Bitterness will strangle the joy out of your relationship with God and with others. You will not love God with all your heart, soul, mind, and strength, and you will certainly not love your neighbor as yourself if you are bitter toward either (see Matthew 6:14-15 and 22:34-40).

James explains how bitterness squeezes the life out of your relationships with one another and with God. He writes:

> Who is wise and understanding among you? By his good conduct let him show his works in the meekness of wisdom. But if you have bitter jealousy and selfish ambition in your hearts, do not boast and be false to the truth. This is not the wisdom that comes down from above, but is earthly, unspiritual, demonic. For where jealousy and selfish ambition exist, there will be disorder and every vile practice. But the wisdom from above is first pure, then peaceable, gentle, open to reason, full of mercy and good fruits, impartial and sincere. And a harvest of righteousness is sown in peace by those who make peace. – James 3:13–18

In the Bible, the word "wisdom" refers to a paradigm for living, or a way of living according to an objective source of knowledge. In the books of Proverbs and Ecclesiastes, wisdom is contrasted with "foolishness" and "folly." In other words, there is a way of living according to wisdom and a way of living according to foolishness.

In the passage above, James indicates that bitter jealousy and selfish ambition—words that betray a heart filled with entitlement—are ways of living. They emerge from a wisdom that is not informed by God and Scripture, "but is earthly, unspiritual, demonic." If your season of life is characterized by bitterness, jealousy, or selfish ambition, you are not living according to the way of God's wisdom, but according to the foolish way of earthly, unspiritual, demonic wisdom. This will necessarily affect your capacity to love others and God in your current season of life.

Embracing the "when" of your spiritual journey involves repentance. Repentance is the volitional and intentional turning away from the foolish, earthy, unspiritual, demonic wisdom by which you are living. Repentance is also volitionally and intentionally turning toward God and His wisdom. Without repentance, the vine of bitterness strengthens its grip.

Bitterness will keep you from journaling because it hardens your heart to notice the subtle loving advances of God. For instance, the Lord may be encouraging you through a friend, but in your bitterness you shrug off the encouragement. Bitterness also floods the content of your journaling such that each page bears witness to your unrepentant, entitled heart. If you are thinking and feeling it, your words will reveal it, too.

Is the "when" of your journaling characterized by an entitled, bitter heart? Will you pause now and repent?

Life Sucker 3: Nostalgia

Sometimes bitterness is veiled under the guise of nostalgia. "The good old days were so wonderful!" Were they really? Do you really want to go back to wearing flip-flops in communal dorm showers? Do you really want to go back to pre-drivers license days with your mommy and daddy driving you around? Do you really want to go back to the "simple" time when you could not read or write or change your own diaper? Do you really want to go back to a time when a "mobile phone" meant getting out of your car and putting quarters into a phone in a booth? Do you really want to use the word "not," watch *Max Headroom* on TV, drink New Coke, or use dial-up modem internet and store data on 1.44 megabyte floppy disks? About the only thing that I would want to go back for is gas under a dollar per gallon.

Like a distracted driver who is texting on his phone, nostalgia mentally and emotionally removes you from the present moment. And, just as texting while driving endangers your life and the lives of those around you, nostalgia puts you in danger of a spiritual crash. Nostalgia offers you an idealized past that is always better in your mind than it was in reality. Nostalgia robs you of joy in your current season of life—the "when" of your journey—even if your current season is full of sorrow, pain, and frustration. Nostalgia is dangerously deceptive.

King Solomon writes a simple proverb in Ecclesiastes that we would do well to take to heart:

> Say not, "Why were the former days better than these?" For it is not from wisdom that you ask this. – Ecclesiastes 7:10

Nostalgia does not come from wisdom. Just as lust is an earthly, unspiritual, demonic mockery of love, nostalgia is a dark version of reflection. In reflection, you consider your past actions and circumstances and attend to how God was involved in them. In nostalgia, you envision a fantastical past and, in so doing, make yourself the god over that false reality. Nostalgia is earthly, unspiritual, demonic.

Nostalgia keeps you from embracing your current spiritual community if you are measuring the people by a nostalgic memory of a previous community. The people in your past community were just as sinful, just as broken, and just as focused on image management as the people in your current community. The difference is that you are idolizing the past at the expense of the present. You are rooted in a fantastical time period instead of the "when" of your journaling today.

Nostalgia will keep you from journaling because your mental and emotional bandwidth is spent on ruminating over a better-than-reality past rather than reflecting on and exploring the present. When I was wrestling through my frustration at Metanoia's slow growth, I found myself thinking about and glorifying past ministry experiences instead of discerning God's activity in the present with Metanoia. After journaling helped me gain perspective and move forward with the church start, I found myself wondering why I had not done it earlier. Nostalgia was the distracting culprit.

The good news is that journaling provides an appropriate avenue to reflect on the past without glorifying it like nostalgia does. When you read your journal entries from months, years, and decades gone by, you get a picture of what your past was actually like. Additionally, as you journal about the memories of days gone by, you can invite the Spirit into your current narrative. You can redeem your nostalgic fantasies by celebrating or mourning a past that is not part of your present.

"When" Are You Today?

Rather than blaming God for the life assigned to us (entitlement), hardening our heart to receiving love from God and others (bitterness), or lamenting for the "good old days" (nostalgia), disciples of Christ are called to live presently in the here and now.

Solomon's father, David, tells us that before you were formed in your mother's womb, God knew every day of your life!

> Your eyes saw my unformed substance;
> in your book were written, every one of
> them, the days that were formed for me,
> when as yet there was none of them. –
> Psalm 139:16

This means that you can (and should) embrace every day as a gift, recognize that God is already in tomorrow, and believe that your season of life is not a curse that you should try to escape. Today is an opportunity to experience redemption in all of your grief and sorrow, joy and victory.

The good news is that journaling is a discipline of reflection, so it can help you embrace your current season of life as a gift from God.

- Journaling helps you combat entitlement by noticing and acknowledging God's active work in your life today—even if it is not as pleasant or fulfilling as you wish it to be.

- Journaling softens your bitter heart by training your eyes to notice God's loving advances even in the most mundane of experiences.

- Journaling releases you from the deceptive grip of nostalgia by opening your eyes to the amazing life God has for you today and the marvelous ways He redeems your past.

Tips for Engaging Journaling "Today"

Here are a couple of journaling tips to resist the life suckers of entitlement, bitterness, and nostalgia while engaging in your season of life today:

- **Acknowledge.** Begin by acknowledging the blessings and limitations of your current season of life. By acknowledging your season of life, you free yourself from unrealistic expectations about journaling. If you are married with children, you cannot stay up until 2:00 am (well, you do that anyway wiping noses and changing diapers), you will have a messy house, and you probably cannot pray and read your Bible while sitting on a blanket next to a river while nursing a chai latte for 2 hours followed by a 30-minute nap.

  Acknowledging also involves putting words to your struggles. If you are single and longing for marriage, explore your desire for marriage and express your longing to the Lord in your journal. Your journaling might just be the door to a breakthrough as you deepen your intimacy with Christ and embrace His plan for your life today.

- **Plan.** Acknowledging is not enough—you must plan ahead to journal. If you have a long commute, you need to wake up earlier, stay up later, or seize your lunch break to journal. If you are married-with-kids, you need to work together with your spouse to help each other find time. If you are single-with-kids, you need to ask friends to step in and give you some space to reflect through journaling. If you are a retired empty nester, you need to discipline yourself to schedule a time for journaling. If you are in college, you need to set aside some time to study your life through reflective journaling.

- **Start.** Have you ever faced a big project at school or work and procrastinated until the last minute to start? Sometimes starting is the hardest part. With regard to journaling, restarting can be even more difficult than starting. Maybe you journaled before and are finding it difficult to restart because you are not sure how to write about everything that happened since your last journal entry. Here is a word of advice: do not worry about what you missed. Just start writing about today. It is better to have written about today in your journal than nothing at all.

- **Practice.** As with any art, skill, or other worthy endeavor, you must practice journaling in order to benefit from it. Turn off the TV, silence the MP3 player, clear your schedule, and start writing. Writing something down is better than not writing anything.

- **Seize.** Sometimes you get an unexpected 10-minute moment here or there. These are opportunities to journal, pray, or otherwise reflect on your life. Keep your journal with you, or use a digital journal or note-taking service on your smartphone (like Evernote) and seize that moment to write. (I carry a miniature softcover Moleskine journal in my back pocket just for this purpose.)

You can do this. Remember, something written down is better than nothing written down. What you write down might catalyze a breakthrough for spiritual freedom in your life today.

In the next chapter I explore the "who" of journaling. After all, it is not just you looking at the page.

Season of Life and Journaling: Dorothy Day (AD 1897-1980)

Dorothy Day is mostly known for her work as a journalist and her social activism. She and Peter Maurin founded the Catholic Worker movement in the 1930s, which blended nonviolence and pacifism to raise awareness and bring aid to the poor and homeless. Day was also instrumental in creating *The Catholic Worker* newspaper, in which she utilized her journalism skills to bring awareness to the social justice concerns of her day.

Day was aware of her season of life and the culture around her. She leveraged her years both as a single adult and when she was married to accomplish the work that God had for her. Day's autobiography, *The Long Loneliness*, chronicles her conversion from a lifestyle that did not glorify God to one of devout faith expressed in missional service of others. Several of her journal entries are reproduced in *On Pilgrimage*, where she recounts the events of her daily life. The insight into the seemingly mundane events of life found in both books serves as an example of how you can cultivate an awareness of God's presence in your season of life today.

Reflection Through Journaling

- Think about your current season of life. How do you describe it?

- Are you living presently in your season of life? If not, what is preventing you from doing so?

- What will you do today to establish a practical rhythm of journaling in your life?

Chapter 5

Jesus: The "Who" of Journaling

How Many Journals?

As I shared in Chapter 3, I periodically get asked questions about how many different types of journals someone should keep. I introduced you to some of the reasons why I believe in a "one-journal life." As you may recall, Colossians 3:1-17 was foundational in helping me understand that all of life is a sacred journey with Christ.

I advocate for a one-journal life because it helps to integrate all aspects of life into one narrative: the sacred journey with Christ. (Not to mention that it simplifies things and saves some cash.) I believe that bifurcating my life into "sacred" and "secular" categories is subjective, arbitrary, and perhaps even unbiblical. This is because all of life for the disciple of Jesus Christ—the sin and the virtue—is part of *one* spiritual journey unique to that individual.

This is not to say that keeping more than one journal is "wrong" or "sinful." You may recall that I used to keep multiple journals at one time. What follows is less an argument for "one" journal than it is a description of "who" journaling is all about. It is through exploring my conviction that journaling is ultimately about Jesus that you will have a greater understanding for why I encourage you to keep one journal.

Sacred Life

We need not look any further than the incarnation of the Son of God to understand that all of life for the believer in Christ is "sacred." John 1:1-18 describes in detail how everything came into existence through Jesus, the eternal, uncreated, Living Word of God. The climax of John's argument is found in verse 14: "And the Word became flesh and dwelt among us, and we have seen his glory, glory as of the only Son from the Father, full of grace and truth."

When Jesus put on flesh, He made human existence "sacred." Thus, when you are inhabited by Jesus through His Holy Spirit, your life takes on the "sacred" characteristic as well. This does not mean that you become God or incapable of sinning like Jesus was in His incarnation. However, it does mean that something is *qualitatively different* about you at the core.

As a disciple of Jesus Christ saved by grace through faith in Him alone, you are a new creation with a new identity on a new journey (see Ephesians 2:1-10).

A New Creation

Paul used the words "new creation" to describe how Jesus' disciples are radically transformed by grace through faith in Christ to become a holy people. In 2 Corinthians, he explains that in and through Christ, disciples are transformed from fleshly people, "secular," to righteous people, "holy" or "sacred."

> From now on, therefore, we regard no one according to the flesh. Even though we once regarded Christ according to the flesh, we regard him thus no longer. Therefore, if anyone is in Christ, he is a new creation. The old has passed away; behold, the new has come. All this is from God, who through Christ reconciled us to himself and gave us the ministry of reconciliation; that is, in Christ God was reconciling the world to himself, not counting their trespasses against them, and entrusting to us the message of reconciliation. Therefore, we are ambassadors for Christ, God making his appeal through us. We implore you on behalf of Christ, be reconciled to God. For our sake he made him to be sin who knew no sin, so that in him we might become the righteousness of God. – 2 Corinthians 5:16-21

This does not mean that Jesus' disciples are incapable of sinning or disobeying God. Quite the contrary—we battle the vestiges of our flesh until the day we die.

I like to think of a chimney to understand this ongoing battle against sinful tendencies. The fire may be quenched and the fuel and ash may be removed from the fireplace, but the soot that lines the chimney—creosote—is flammable and dangerous. For the disciple of Christ, the fire and fuel of sin are removed by Jesus' atoning death on the cross and victorious resurrection from the grave.

However, the creosote of the flesh—that part of you that is bent by sin—remains until the final cleansing upon Christ's return or your death, whichever comes first. Your life, then, becomes one of battling against the creosote of your flesh through Christ's empowering grace (see Romans 8). Thus, even the battle waged against sin is part of the "sacred" journey.

A New Identity

What this means is that your position in Christ is not determined by your relative "goodness" or "badness." In fact, those terms lose their meaning once you are transformed by grace. It is Christ who determines your identity, and it is your identity that determines your position with God.

Peter explains that this new identity is so sweeping that believers in Christ are literally an entirely different people on earth:

> But you are a chosen race, a royal
> priesthood, a holy nation, a people for his
> own possession, that you may proclaim
> the excellencies of him who called you out
> of darkness into his marvelous light. Once
> you were not a people, but now you are
> God's people; once you had not received
> mercy, but now you have received mercy.
> – 1 Peter 2:9–10

Because Christ dwells within you, you are "holy" or "sacred" even as you wage war against the pollution of your flesh. Peter acknowledges this reality and describes it in terms of a pilgrimage between earth and heaven, an exile while waiting to go Home (see 1 Peter 2:11-12).

So comprehensive is this new identity reality that Paul writes in Romans 8:10: "But if Christ is in you, although the body is dead because of sin, the Spirit is life because of righteousness." Your life is literally one lived in the Spirit and defined by righteousness when Christ saves you.

A New Journey

It is your new creation and identity in Christ that makes all of life "spiritual" and "sacred." This is because Christ inhabits you by His Holy Spirit. Do you remember from Chapter 3 how I referenced Colossians 3:1-4, where Paul says that Christ *is* your life? The indwelling Holy Spirit is how this marvelous truth is possible!

Since Christ *is* your life, each day is part of a new, sacred journey. We will explore this journey more fully in Chapter 7. In the meantime, consider this amazing truth: as a believer in Jesus Christ, your life *is* a sacred journey *in* Christ. *It really is!* Maybe you need to pause right now and reflect on this amazing truth. Go ahead—grab your pen and journal.

* * *

Because life in Christ is sacred, all of the stuff of everyday life, of spiritual ruminations, of poetry and music, of romance and friendship, and of achievements and academics are sacred. Whether or not you keep one journal like me or multiple journals, it is more important that you understand and believe that your life is sacred because of, through, and in Christ.

Hopefully you now understand that journaling is ultimately more about Jesus than it is about you. With this as our foundational thought, I will briefly share with you my story of how I made the decision to keep one journal.

Journaling and the Sacred Journey

At one point in time while in college I actually kept four journals:

- **Red Journal.** I dubbed this the "Red Journal" because it was red. I know, creative, right? The Red Journal was a record of my daily life. I wrote about how play rehearsals were going, thoughts on my romantic interests, how I was dealing with a season of depression, and other ruminations on college life.

- **Spiritual Journal.** This journal bore the name "Spiritual Journal" because it included notes from sermons that I listened to, prayers that I wrote out to God, and ruminations from my daily "quiet time" with the Lord. Another creative name, eh?

- **City Lights Journal.** While visiting San Francisco in the summer after my junior year, I picked up a journal at City Lights Bookstore. City Lights was the hub of the Beat Movement that produced writers like Alan Ginsberg, Lawrence Ferlinghetti, and Jack Kerouac, among others. What better journal to record my poetic ramblings and songs that I wrote? I get no creative points for the name of this journal as it was bequeathed from the location where I purchased it.

- **Senior Project Journal.** I was looking down the barrel at three senior projects at the beginning of my senior year. One for my English major (creative writing emphasis), one for my Communication Arts major, and one for the Honors Program. Thankfully, my advisors got on board with my idea to accomplish all three requirements with one project: writing, directing, and producing a two-act play. I captured the beautiful chaos of that season in a journal dedicated to my senior project. A creative season of my life despite the pragmatic name for this journal.

Shortly after college I wanted to live in a way that reflected the sacred journey of my new creation, new identity, and new journey in Christ. This is why I began keeping two journals: one for my poetry and one for anything and everything else. Even though I moved from four to two journals, I still did not feel like my journaling practice reflected what I knew to be the reality of my sacred life. Therefore, a couple of years after my decision to keep two journals, I began keeping only one.

Remember, journaling is less about me ("who") and more about Jesus ("Who"). Yes, I may be writing about my kids battling a stomach bug, my frustration over replacing the water heater, or my hopes and dreams, but remember: Jesus is involved in my day-to-day rhythm. Every word that you and I pen is a description of life with Christ. And, if you and I choose to reflect upon what we write, we will inevitably find Jesus on every page.

Tips for Journaling the Journey

As an expression of my conviction that journaling is ultimately more about Jesus than it is about me, I write the following on the inside cover of every journal: the date I began the journal, the date I completed the journal, and the phrases "An Exposition of Life Lived" and "A Sacred Journey."

You may choose to write something similar to reflect your own conviction that all of life is a sacred journey in Christ.

This great theological truth means that every moment of every day is an opportunity for fellowship with Jesus. Here are some tips for how you can encounter Jesus in and through reflecting on your sacred journey through journaling:

- **Big things.** Journal about the "big" things—decisions about where to work, who to marry, amazing encounters with God, deep moments of grief and sorrow, etc.

- **Small potatoes.** Write about the "small" stuff, too. If you only journal during seasons of great decision making, rejoicing, and mourning, then your journal will reflect a lopsided view of your life. The small things are actually the nuances of life with Christ. They are the dash of salt that makes the chocolate chip cookie irresistible. Write about how your day went, what you are reading, what the weather was like today, how you are battling a cold, etc.

- **Routine check-up.** Every six to eight weeks, I turn back the pages of my journal and reflect. I look for emerging themes in my life, recurring sins I am struggling against, and ways the Lord is making Himself known to me. Each journal entry serves as a guidepost or a lighthouse guiding me along in my spiritual journey. Whether you review every six weeks, quarterly, or annually, keep up this practice and you will find it is much simpler (not necessarily easier) to make significant decisions because you see the direction God is taking your life.

- **Annual evaluation.** I wish that I were better at doing this. For a couple of years every December I wrote a brief annual evaluation—what I called a "chapter"—summarizing the year. Combing through my journals and writing down what happened in my life over the previous twelve months was amazing. I really have no excuse and I probably should pick up this practice again.

- **His Word before mine.** When Kim was in college, she developed a principle to help ensure that her journaling focused on her sacred journey with Christ: "His Word before mine." If she began to sense that her journaling was too "me-focused" (her phrase), Kim would read her Bible before journaling, copy a verse from what she read into her journal, and then reflect on how it applied to her life.

The "who" of journaling is not just about you and Jesus. There are other people who share your sacred journey to some degree or other. Here are some tips for reflecting on the role your social network, influences, and spiritual community has in your spiritual journey.

- **Influences.** The last page of my journal is always dedicated to a list of the books that I read while I kept that particular journal. I write down the book title, the author's name, and the month that I finished reading this book. This helps me to understand who and what influenced my thinking and development over the course of keeping the journal.

- **Intercession.** The two or three pages preceding the last page of my journal is dedicated to listing out people who I pray for: family members, church members, and lost persons. Writing down updates such as answers to prayer or setbacks helps my prayer life develop.

In the next chapter I explore the "where" of journaling: ways you can integrate journaling into other spiritual disciplines.

Jesus and Journaling: St. Augustine (AD 354-430)

Many autobiographies and other personal narratives written by believers read a lot like journals since they detail a person's journey with Christ. St. Augustine's *Confessions* is one example of an autobiography that has journal-like qualities. Augustine's reflections in *Confessions* share similar characteristics to what you might record in your journal as you reflect on your own sacred journey.

In *Confessions*, Augustine, the Archbishop of Hippo, details his conversion from a luxurious and lewd lifestyle to passionate followership of Jesus Christ. We gain insight into Augustine's interior world—his thoughts, doubts, and convictions—as he describes his spiritual journey. The pages of *Confessions* describe his life as a new creation with a new identity on a new journey with Christ.

Reflection Through Journaling

- What must you do today to live a more integrated life in Christ?

- We discussed the implications of life in/with/ through Christ on journaling. What are the implications of this reality on prayer, Scripture reading, sharing your faith, missions, worship, dating, marriage, and parenting?

- Who do you know in your neighborhood, school, workplace, home, or church that would benefit from hearing the Good News of life in Christ today? What will you do to make sure they hear about it?

Chapter 6

Discipline: The "Where" of Journaling

Not Another Living Soul

It was March 2003. I made my way to the mountains of North Carolina to stay in a secluded cabin for three nights by myself. After picking up groceries for my stay, I had no contact with any other human being for the three-night, four-day stay. I did not even use a phone to call friends or family.

I went to the mountains to discern vocational direction. On the one hand, I was given an opportunity to transition my pastoral responsibilities from student ministry to worship and arts ministry at the church that I was serving in Georgia. On the other hand, there was an opportunity to move to Maryland and begin planting what is now called Metanoia Church. While on the mountaintop, God clearly led me to stay in Georgia and transition my pastoral duties from students to worship and arts. He also assured me that some day I would move to Maryland to start Metanoia.

Another reason why I went to the mountains was a bit more personal. I was in my mid-twenties and getting ready to graduate from seminary. I had gone on maybe four or five dates in as many years and was very discontented with being a single adult. I desired marriage at my core. While on the mountaintop, God assured me that He was in control, that He was aware of my desires, that my desire for marriage was a good thing, and that He was sufficient for me in whatever season of life I found myself.

One week after that solitude retreat, I got in touch with my contacts in Maryland and told them that I would not be coming up to plant Metanoia that summer. One month after the retreat, I transitioned between the two ministries at our church in Georgia. Five months after the retreat, I met my wife, Kim, in a local coffee shop. Two-and-a-half years after that same retreat, Kim and I packed up our belongings, moved to Maryland, celebrated our first anniversary, and began planting Metanoia.

There was no profound mysterious voice coming from a burning bush that told me exactly what to do. In reality, I brought about one dozen journals with me and poured over them for those four days. I made note of themes, recurring Scripture references, and ways God spoke to me through sermons, mentors, and books as far back as high school.

Within a few days on that mountaintop, I had a clear "map" of where God had taken me over the years and where it appeared that He was leading me in the coming years. This is how I made my decision to "stay" and transition ministry leadership in Georgia, to "wait" and prepare better for Metanoia, and to experience contentment as a single adult before I met Kim.

"Where" Journaling Helps

The "where" of journaling involves integrating journaling and other spiritual disciplines to aid in making decisions and to catalyze your spiritual growth. In other words, journaling serves the purpose of helping you determine "where" you have been, "where" you are today, and "where" you are going in your spiritual journey.

The story above illustrates how journaling helped me make a significant vocational decision. Reflection through journaling helps you to see the context of your decision—it is never just about the moment. By looking backward, you can look forward to make decisions.

The story above also illustrates how journaling complemented the disciplines of solitude and prayer to help me find contentment in Christ. Spiritual disciplines are tools that aid you to go "where" the Spirit is taking you. Just as you would not use a hammer to drive in a screw, so, too, spiritual disciplines are employed to address your unique place in life. That place is "where" you find yourself today.

There are several ways integrating journaling with other spiritual disciplines facilitates this journey, but for the purposes of this chapter, we will explore three primary categories:

- Disciplines of the Word

- Disciplines of Prayer

- Disciplines of Reflection

I explore decision-making under the Disciplines of Reflection category below.

Disciplines of the Word

Disciplines of the Word are perhaps the most immediate category of spiritual disciplines to integrate with journaling. Disciplines of the Word include things like Bible study, meditation, Scripture memory, *Lectio Divina*, devotional readings, and sermon notes. As a way of introducing the idea of integrating journaling with disciplines of the Word, we will look at only two disciplines of the Word: Bible study and sermon notes.

Journaling and Bible Study

You should have your journal with you whenever you study Scripture at home, on retreat, or in a Bible study class. When studying the Bible on your own, here are four important things to integrate into your journaling. Sometimes all four of these show up in a single journal entry, but often there are only one, two, or three of them present. The four things are easily remembered using the acronym S.O.A.P. I first learned about S.O.A.P. in a sermon preached by Wayne Corderio, but I cannot remember when or where I heard it.

- **Scripture: *What did you read?*** As we fill our minds with the truth of Scripture, it transforms us and enables us to live the life God desires us to live. Simply write down the Scripture reference for what you read that day. For example, "John 1-3" or "Psalm 139." This facilitates renewing your mind with God's Word.

   "Do not be conformed to this world, but be transformed by the renewal of your mind, that by testing you may discern what is the will of God, what is good and acceptable and perfect." – Romans 12:1-2

- **Observation: *What did you observe?*** Write down your observations of what you are reading. You may also choose to write out a verse or two that the Holy Spirit seems to be impressing upon you that day. Recording your observation helps you reflect on what you are reading as you meditate on the Word.

   "I will meditate on your precepts and fix my eyes on your ways." – Psalm 119:15

- **Application: *What one thing will I do to apply this immediately?*** What we read and observe we are meant to obey and put into practice (see James 1:22-25). I am a fan of simplicity, so discipline yourself to identify only *one* way to apply the text to your life *immediately*.

  "But be doers of the word, and not hearers only, deceiving yourselves." – James 1:22

- **Prayer: *What is my response to God?*** God has spoken to you, so now respond back to Him in prayer. Remember, this is a two-way relationship. Consider writing out a brief prayer in your journal.

  "I hasten and do not delay to keep your commandments." – Psalm 119:60

Journaling helps us to apply the Word of God and to experience God speaking to us through His Word. This is also true when we keep sermon notes.

Journaling and Sermon Notes

Did you know that preaching and receiving the preached Word of God are both acts of worship? If the preacher reduces preaching to merely giving information or the listener reduces preaching to merely receiving information, the act of preaching is reduced to an academic, religious, or philosophical endeavor. In reality, God speaks to us through preaching, and our active response to the preaching is an act of worship (see Romans 10:13-15). Journaling helps us attend to what God is saying through the preacher and serves as a record of our response for future reflection.

The following are some ways that you can worship God through taking sermon notes. They are easily remembered using the acronym D.O.O.R.:

- **Details.** Write down the important details about the sermon preached, such as the date, the preacher's name, the title of the sermon, and the Scripture reference(s).

- **Outline.** Discipline yourself to follow the "flow" of the sermon by identifying the outline of the sermon. Sometimes preachers will give you a printed outline, such as sermon notes, that can easily be recorded in your journal. Other times, the preacher may give audible cues to help you follow the sermon, such as phrases like "here is my next point" or "here is the third way to apply this." Identify the preacher's primary or main point.

- **Observation.** While listening to a sermon, you should be observing three persons. The first person is yourself: What is going on inside of you as you listen to the sermon? Are you open to receiving this Word? Why or why not? The second person is the preacher: What does he appear to be most passionate about in his sermon? The third and most important person is the Holy Spirit: What is the Spirit saying to you?

- **Respond.** In order for listening to a sermon to truly be an act of worship, you must respond to the Holy Spirit. Journaling facilitates recording your worshipful response. Consider asking: How will I apply the Word preached today in the coming days?

Unfortunately, most of what we hear in a sermon is forgotten by the next morning if not by Sunday night. Can you relate? What was the topic, Scripture reference, and main point of the most recent sermon you listened to? What did God say to you through the sermon and how have you applied His Word since listening to the sermon? Journaling not only opens the D.O.O.R. to worship, but also helps us to recall God's truths at a later date.

Disciplines of Prayer

God is always speaking to you. Always. Right now. Do you believe this? Disciplines of prayer—such as intercession, fasting, fixed-hour prayer, church prayer gatherings, and praying through prayer books—tune our ears to the voice of God.

As we write out our prayers or record our prayer concerns, we keep a record of ways that God answers prayer or redirects the conversation. We also have a record of our deepening understanding of prayer as a conversation with God.

Here are some ways you can leverage your journal to help you grow in the disciplines of prayer:

- **Make a list.** Record a list of prayer requests. I keep a list of every member in our church in the back pocket of my Moleskine journal and pray over it regularly. I also keep a list of friends, family, and neighbors who are not yet believers in Jesus Christ. Scattered throughout my journals are lists of prayer concerns for my family, my church, and myself. These lists help me be intentional in my intercession and petition.

- **Check it twice.** One advantage of keeping a list of prayer requests is that you can record the date when God answered that prayer. By the way, "no" and "not now" are also ways that God answers prayer in addition to "yes." When you write down the "yes," "no," and "not now" answers to prayer, you begin to understand God's desires for your life, mission, and ministry.

- **Make it conversational.** Consider writing out your prayers if your mind tends to wander while you pray. This will help you stay focused and lend an element of intentionality to your prayer. Journal your prayer conversationally: "Father, my mind is wandering right now. I really want to commune with You in prayer. As I pen these words in my journal, please guide me to pray for what is in Your heart for my life and our world today."

- **Check on distractions.** By the way, your mental and emotional "distractions" are not merely "distractions." They distract you because they are important to you. You are thinking about TV shows, calendars, stressors, people, and dreams because they matter to you. Rather than berating yourself for thinking about these distractions, jot them down in your journal and ask for God's perspective on them. You may find more direction in your schedule and you may consume less media.

Start journaling as you pray and you will grow through the spiritual disciplines of prayer.

Disciplines of Reflection

The third category is disciplines of reflection. The story at the beginning of this chapter already illustrated how journaling integrates well with another reflective discipline: solitude. For the purposes of this section, I will explore integrating journaling with reflective decision-making.

Often times, making decisions can lead to sleepless nights and obsessive thinking. Journaling can enable you to get out of your head and gain perspective. It allows you to be more intentional in how you process your decision-making.

Reflecting on what you have written over the course of weeks, months, years, and decades helps you to identify guideposts or lighthouses along the way. Just like rowing a rowboat, it is by looking backward that you move forward. In this way, journaling facilitates decision-making.

Here are some questions to ask as you review your past journal entries when making decisions:

- What Scriptures seem to be important to me lately?

- How did God lead me in similar decisions in the past?

- What similar situations have I faced in the past, and what did I learn from them by making wise or foolish decisions?

Here are some questions to ask and record in your journal when making decisions:

- How does God's Word directly and clearly address this decision?

- If God's Word does not clearly address this decision, what principles can I draw from Scripture?

- What is the counsel of those in spiritual authority over me?

- What is the counsel of those in spiritual community with me?

- Does it appear that God is leaving this decision open for my own opinion or decision-making? (If so, create a list of pros and cons to see the big picture of your decision.)

I suggest that you journal your responses to these questions (or similar questions) so that you have a written testimony of how God led you to discern His will.

In the next chapter we will explore the "way" of journaling: cultivating a life of reflection and spiritual growth.

Discipline and Journaling: Lancelot Andrewes (AD 1555-1626)

Few believers today are familiar with Lancelot Andrewes, but they are very familiar with one of his greatest accomplishments. Andrews, a prominent bishop in the Church of England, served as a counselor to King James and was the lead translator of the Authorized Version of the English Bible, or as we are more familiar with it today, the King James Version (KJV). While you may not know of Andrewes, you have most likely benefited from his work translating the KJV.

Andrewes wrote a small book called *Private Devotions*. He used *Devotions* to encourage his prayer and meditation, and never meant for it to be published. In this way, *Devotions* served as a journal that both inspired and bolstered his faith in Christ. Before he died, Andrewes gave *Devotions* to a good friend of his, Archbishop Laud. Eventually, *Devotions* was published and is a treasure trove of prayers rich in theology and praise to God.

Devotions serves as a fine example of a journal leveraged to record and catalyze personal communion with the Lord through prayer. Written prayers—whether in your journal or in prayer books—help you maintain focus when your thoughts wander while praying.

Reflection Through Journaling

- How aware and confident are you with regard to "where" you are spiritually, emotionally, mentally, and physically? What role can journaling play in helping you understand "where" you are?

- In what way will you integrate your journaling with disciplines of the Word this week?

- How will your disciplines of prayer benefit from integrating them with journaling?

- Is there space in your life for reflection? If not, when will you schedule time this week to journal as a discipline of reflection?

Chapter 7

Reflection: The "Way" of Journaling

Crossroads

My absolute favorite book of the Bible is Jeremiah. He is the prophet with the ministry that no one wants. His ministry included proclaiming God's imminent discipline on Judah through the Babylonian army, experiencing firsthand the invasion of Jerusalem, witnessing the horrific razing of the temple and of the city, and then going into the Babylonian exile along with the people of Judah. Jeremiah's experience was so awful that he wrote a book of the Bible called "Lamentations." Not many seminarians today are itching for this kind of ministry assignment!

In the midst of God speaking His prophesies against Judah through Jeremiah, He explains how this horrific crisis could have been avoided:

> Thus says the Lord: "Stand by the roads, and look, and ask for the ancient paths, where the good way is; and walk in it, and find rest for your souls." But they said, "We will not walk in it." – Jeremiah 6:16

The "Way" of God is one that is ancient, good, and full of rest. When Judah refused to walk with God in His "Way," they rejected the Divine for the idol, the ancient for the trendy, the good for the bad, the peace for the pain, and rest for chaos.

This is my favorite verse in all of Scripture primarily because it is more than Judah's story. They were not the first and certainly not the last people to reject God and His Way. It is the story of how every person—you and I included—reject God's loving overtures. You see, we all stand at the crossroads between two ways.

Let's explore Jeremiah 6:16 as a way of introducing you to a lifestyle marked by contemplative reflection. The "Way" of journaling is a way of living contemplatively.

Stand

Reflection begins with standing at the crossroads: stop, be still, and consider the two different ways before you.

Jesus said that it is actually possible to gain all that we seek in this world and lose everything:

> And he said to all, "If anyone would come after me, let him deny himself and take up his cross daily and follow me. For whoever would save his life will lose it,

but whoever loses his life for my sake will save it. For what does it profit a man if he gains the whole world and loses or forfeits himself?" – Luke 9:23-25

In a mysterious paradox, it is by dying to self and the ways of the world and living to Christ that you find life. Jesus essentially says that there are two ways to live: one Way is to live for Christ and the other way is to live for anyone and anything else.

Paul echoes this idea when, in Romans, he introduces two ways of living:

For those who live according to the flesh set their minds on the things of the flesh, but those who live according to the Spirit set their minds on the things of the Spirit. For to set the mind on the flesh is death, but to set the mind on the Spirit is life and peace. For the mind that is set on the flesh is hostile to God, for it does not submit to God's law; indeed, it cannot. Those who are in the flesh cannot please God. – Romans 8:5-8

When you live according to the "way" of the world and the flesh, your reward is death. When you live according to the Way of the Spirit, your reward is life and peace.

Walking in the way of the world and the flesh means losing Jerusalem, losing your soul, and losing your life. Walking in God's Way means discovering Heaven, saving your life, and experiencing peace.

Look

Stand and look. God's Way is ancient. God's Way is good. God's Way is life. God's Way is peace. God's Way is Jesus Christ: "*I am* the way..." (John 14:6).

Encountering Jesus, surrendering to Him, trusting in His atoning sacrifice on the cross, and believing in His victorious resurrection from the dead sets our feet along the Way today and eternally. This is salvation!

As simple as the profound truth of salvation is, it is difficult for many people to grasp. Pride, lust for power, and ignorance of the knowledge of salvation keep many people from receiving this simple, free gift of salvation. Thus, looking involves reflecting on the cost of discipleship to Christ.

Jesus explained that God's Way is difficult:

> Enter by the narrow gate. For the gate is wide and the way is easy that leads to destruction, and those who enter by it are many. For the gate is narrow and the way is hard that leads to life, and those who find it are few. – Matthew 7:13-14

The Way is difficult, but difficulty is not the same as impossible. When you walk with Jesus along His Way, He leads you, guides you, empowers you, and disciplines you so that you will ultimately come to the narrow gate of Heaven *with Him*. Remember, Jesus *is* the Way (He is also the "gate"—see John 10:1-18).

His way is also narrow, but that is not the same as closed. By believing in Jesus and confessing faith in Him, *anyone* can have access to the ancient, good Way of God:

> ...if you confess with your mouth that Jesus is Lord and believe in your heart that God raised him from the dead, you will be saved. For with the heart one believes and is justified, and with the mouth one confesses and is saved. For the Scripture says, "Everyone who believes in him will not be put to shame." For there is no distinction between Jew and Greek; for the same Lord is Lord of all, bestowing his riches on all who call on him. For "everyone who calls on the name of the Lord will be saved." – Romans 10:9-13

Your journals may record months, years, and decades of life lived along the broad way of destruction, but by grace, today you can literally turn the page for a fresh start along God's Way.

Ask

Faith in Christ is a pilgrimage and spiritual growth is a journey along the narrow, hard Way that leads to life. This journey involves deciding daily to walk the Way (stand, look) and then actually putting forth the effort to walk along the Way (ask, walk). The spiritual fruit is all in God's hand (you will find rest).

As we read in Chapter 2, M. Robert Mulholland, Jr. explains that spirituality is a journey or a pilgrimage. You may recall that he says, "Spiritual formation is a process of being conformed to the image of Christ for the sake of others."[9] This idea of spiritual pilgrimage is captured in the images of the "good way" and the "narrow way" in the passages above.

Mulholland further explains why understanding spiritual growth as a journey is so important:

> When spirituality is viewed as a static possession, the way to spiritual wholeness is seen as the acquisition of information and techniques that enable us to gain possession of the desired state of spirituality. Discipleship is perceived as "my" spiritual life and tends to be defined by actions that ensure its possession. Thus the endless quest for techniques, methods, programs by which we hope to "achieve" spiritual fulfillment.

The hidden premise behind all of this is the unquestioned assumption that we alone are in control of our spirituality. In brief, we assume we are in control of our relationship with God.

When spirituality is viewed as a journey, however, the way to spiritual wholeness is seen to lie in an increasingly faithful response to the One whose purpose shapes our path, whose grace redeems our detours, whose power liberates us from crippling bondages of the prior journey and whose transforming presence meets us at each turn in the road. In other words, holistic spirituality is a pilgrimage of deepening responsiveness to God's control of our life and being.[10]

Mulholland rejects the idea that life along the Way can be reduced to formulas, mantras, and techniques. This was the error that Judah made when they rejected the messy unpredictable nature of faith in the living God for the predictable and controllable worship of idols. This is the same error that the Jewish Scribes and Pharisees made centuries later when they rejected faith in the Messiah (Christ).

Asking is the first movement of effort along the spiritual journey. It is as you ask Christ for salvation, faith, help, freedom, grace, deliverance, love, and endurance that you progress along the way. This is why Mulholland says "spiritual wholeness is...an increasingly faithful response" to Jesus. You must ask for help along God's Way. You must exercise absolute dependence upon and surrender to God.

And, you must walk.

Walk

You are never alone along the Way. Christ is with you, and so are other pilgrims past, present, and yet to come.

For centuries, our brothers and sisters in Christ have traveled along the Way through prayer, meditation, Bible study, preaching, worship, confession, spiritual friendship, spiritual direction, fasting, solitude, simplicity, Sabbath, silence, examen, *Lectio Divina*, and countless other spiritual disciplines. These disciplines of the Word, prayer, and reflection are the intentional activities you engage along the Way to grow in your faith. They are how you "walk" in the Way.

Journaling is part of the great repertoire of these ancient, trustworthy activities that facilitate the deepening of our relationship with God and our spiritual transformation along the Way. Journaling shares the unique and strategic purpose of other reflective spiritual disciplines. You may find these other reflective disciplines helpful along the Way:

- **Solitude.** As a disciple of Christ, you are never really alone even in solitude. Solitude as a reflective discipline helps you to identify internal longings and fears, and to listen to the still, small voice of God.

- **Sabbath.** There is a reason why God commanded His people to observe a weekly Sabbath and why Jesus declared that He is the Lord of the Sabbath (see Exodus 20:8-11; Deuteronomy 5:12-15; and Matthew 12:1-8). It is because ceasing from work for one entire day out of the week for the purpose of reflecting on your journey with Christ is life-giving. It is as you cease that you physically declare: "Jesus, you are Lord, and I am not!"

- **Spiritual direction.** A spiritual director helps you listen to the Holy Spirit, to reflect on what the Spirit is saying, and to respond to the Spirit.

- **Daily examen.** What is your routine when you go to bed? Do you reflect on the day? Practicing the ancient discipline of examen is a wonderful way to reflect on the daily movement of God in your life. Consider reflecting on the following: Where did you encounter Christ? When did you need Christ? Did you disappoint Him? How does His grace cover your sin?

In addition to journaling, there is one other reflective discipline that has a tremendous impact on my spiritual formation. I do not really know what to call this discipline, so I will simply describe it to you. It is the act of collecting rocks to remind me of significant moments of communion with God.

I drove over a creek to get back to the main road while on my way down from the mountain of solitude in 2003. After crossing the creek I pulled my truck over, jumped out, fished a rock out of the creek, and tossed it in my truck bed. Every time I look at that rock it reminds me of the life-transforming days kept with God in solitude. Perhaps, as with the Israelites and myself, rocks may serve you as another way that you can intentionally reflect on life along the Way.

Choosing the Way

I spent the bulk of this chapter exploring my favorite verse of Scripture, Jeremiah 6:16, to introduce you to the Way of journaling. Here now is my expanded paraphrase: *Stand at the crossroads and look at the two ways before you. One way is the good, ancient Way of God and His people. It is the Way of the Spirit—and the Way is, in fact, Christ. The other way is the broad, easy journey of the world and the flesh. Ask God to show you by His grace which one is the good, ancient, Christ Way. Then, make the choice and walk in it. For, it is as you walk—applying your effort through spiritual disciplines to cooperate with the Spirit's transforming power—that you will, in fact, find rest for your soul. And this is not meant to end with you, but is for the sake of others.*

Standing, looking, asking, walking, and resting is the Way of journaling! Could there be any journey more inspiring, all-encompassing, adventurous, fulfilling, or dangerous as this? That is not a rhetorical question. The answer is "no!"

Stand at the crossroads. Look. Ask for the good, ancient Way. Which way will you walk?

It is easy to walk the broad way—to live a life full of activity and no reflection, to passively consume media and not actively meditate on the Word of God, to feed the flesh and not discipline it.

Even though I have been on pilgrimage along the Way for many decades now, I still periodically choose to wander into the rhythms of the broad way. It is by God's grace and my meager efforts applied through spiritual disciplines in cooperation with the Spirit that I continue along the narrow way with the Way.

Journaling along the Way provides a record of where you have been—valleys, mountaintops, dark forests, shimmering rivers, arid plateaus, lush meadows, endless oceans, epic vistas—and helps you discern where the Good

Shepherd (see John 10) is leading you in the coming days. It is a record of your victories and your setbacks, your starts and stops. It is a sacred record of a life spent in company with God.

Well, now that I think about it, a journal is probably not really your story or my story at all. It seems to me that it is Someone Else's story, and that makes all the difference in the world for what happens between the pages.

Reflection and Journaling: J. B. Phillips (AD 1906-1982)

John Bertram Phillips, a contemporary of C. S. Lewis, wrote several books that encouraged the faith of millions. Phillips lived in a time when liberal scholarship attacked many orthodox beliefs of the Bible and Christian doctrine in general. His books helped many believers in Great Britain, the United States of America, and Canada counter the liberal wave of scholarship. Phillips is perhaps most known for his translation of the New Testament in contemporary vernacular.

Many of his contemporaries were not aware of Phillip's lifelong struggle with depression and anxiety. At times, the darkness was so heavy upon him that he had to cancel book signings and speaking engagements. After his death, Phillips' wife, Vera, along with a good friend, Edwin Robertson, published *J. B. Phillips: The Wounded Healer*. *The Wounded Healer* is a collection of excerpts from letters and journal entries that provide a window into Phillips' journey through the emotional, mental, and spiritual darkness of depression and anxiety. For those of us who struggle with similar anguish, this short book serves as an example of how a journal can help us process our pain and seek healing in the Lord.

Reflection Through Journaling

- Which way best describes your spiritual journey? The broad way of the world and the flesh, or the narrow Way of Christ?

- How does your journal tell the story of God's faithfulness in your life along the Way?

- How can journaling help you to stand and look, to discern God's Way for your life?

Conclusion

It's "Okay" if You Struggle

Journaling is not for everyone, but you will never know if you do not give it a fighting chance. Journaling may be hard at first, so please do not throw in the towel too quickly.

You can expect journaling to be difficult for many reasons. For instance, journaling takes a chunk of time, so you may initially resist letting go of something in order to start journaling. Journaling is also highly reflective, and this may bring up some difficult or disturbing thoughts that you have previously been afraid to acknowledge. Journaling is also a means to catalyze spiritual growth, so you can expect the enemy, Satan and his emissaries, to throw every kind of distraction at you and to whisper every sort of "reasonable" excuse for why you "cannot" journal today.

Just sit down and start writing. If your environment at home or work is too distracting, journal in your car for a few minutes or visit a local park or coffee shop. Keep your journal by your bed and write a couple of sentences before you go to sleep each night. Ask a spiritual friend to check in with you once a week. Only, make sure she asks you about the *quality* of your journaling and not the *quantity*.

As with any discipline, stick with it for a significant period of time so that it becomes a healthy habit. As with any other art, "practice makes perfect"—or, in this case, at least "proficient!"

If you give it an intentional and consistent go and journaling just does not seem to work out for you, that is fine. There are many ways to reflect on your spiritual journey other than journaling. Circle back to Chapter 7 and explore the reflective disciplines listed there.

Going Deeper

Do you want to go deeper into the spiritual discipline of journaling? Here are two final suggestions for you:

- First, go to the *Journaling* page on my blog and join the conversation with myself and others. This page is devoted to exploring the concepts in this book and providing a community to share with others your tips and observations related to journaling. You can find it here: http://www.adamlfeldman.com/journaling/

- Second, and most importantly, enjoy this discipline. It is so much fun once you get the hang of it. Relax and do not stress yourself out with journaling. Remember, there is no "right" or "wrong" way to journal.

Grab your pen and join me in journaling our sacred journeys in Christ! If I do not meet you along the Way in this life, I will greet you when we get Home.

Appendix 1

Setting Up a Moleskine Journal

While my journal keeping is relatively casual, I do have a system for setting up my Moleskine journal before I write in it. What you read in this appendix was developed organically over the course of several years of journaling.

Here is how I set up a standard-sized, 240-page unlined hardback Moleskine journal.

Front Matter

- **Quotations.** I reserve the inside of the front cover (in a Moleskine journal, this is where the "www.moleskine.com" website address is printed) for quotations. These are usually passages of Scripture and quotes from books that are very important to me during the time I keep the journal.

- **Front page.** I rarely fill out the "In case of loss, please return to..." section of the front page. However, on the same page I do write the following in the blank space:

An Exposition of Life Lived

A Sacred Journey

Date and time I begin the journal

Date and time I finish the journal

My name

City, State Zip Code

Navigation

- **Pagination.** After I set up my front matter, I number the entire journal. In order to save time, I only write the odd numbers on the bottom right corner of the right page. Numbering the pages in my journal helps me when I do a periodic six-week check-up because I can reference specific page numbers. This aids in navigation, since the length of entries always varies.

- **Opening summary.** On page 1, I write a paragraph summary of my life at the time. I usually include my age and the ages of Kim, Abby, and Joshua as well as the location where I started the journal. Other things that I write include how many years I have been married to Kim, defining life moments such as education milestones, and defining vocational moments such as current mission and vision initiatives within our church.

Closing Pages

- **Prayer list.** I reserve page 239 (and sometimes page 238) to list prayer requests. This list includes the names and prayer concerns of church planters that I am coaching, persons that I am spiritually directing, and lost friends and family members.

- **Book list.** I reserve page 240 to list the books that I read while I kept the journal. It is generally a mix of fiction and non-fiction. I record the title of the book, the name of the author, and the month/year I finished the book.

- **Post-It notes.** The page to the right of page 240 is of thicker paper stock. I line this page with Post-It notes, which come in handy. For instance, when I am meeting with people and need to write something down for them, I have an easily accessible means in my journal. I also use them to scratch out grocery and shopping lists. They are easily replaced and are useful to keep around.

Back Cover

- **Photos.** On the other side of the Post-It note page and on the Moleskine pocket I tape photos. These are often photos of Kim and the kids. My current photos include (1) a photo of me when I wrestled in high school with a motivational phrase that I came up with last year to inspire me while writing this book and (2) a photo of Kim and me on the day I graduated with my doctoral degree.

- **Pocket.** The Moleskine pocket is very helpful to keep important items that you may not wish to keep permanently in your journal. However, you have to be careful, because if you stuff it too thickly, it will warp the shape of your journal and make writing difficult. Here are things that I keep in my pocket: a photo of my family, two business cards, two cards for Metanoia Church, and a list of Metanoia's Partners ("members") so that I can pray for them.

- **Cover.** Occasionally I will affix stickers onto the front and back covers. There are also companies that will "print" designs onto the cover of a new Moleskine. The printing process involves burning off the black layer of the cover to expose the brownish-tan material beneath. It actually looks pretty cool. When I roasted coffee for a local coffee shop, a friend of mine surprised me with a Moleskine journal with a printed design that he created just for me. (We had this running joke between the two of us where he would say: "Don't burn the beans!" while we hung out when I roasted coffee.)

This is how I set up my Moleskine journal. If you are a fan of Moleskine and use their products as well, I would love to learn from you about how you set up your journal!

Appendix 2

Making a Plan to Journal

Maybe the thought of starting (or restarting) journaling is a bit overwhelming, or maybe you need some space to think a bit more about how you will be more intentional in your journaling. This appendix helps you craft a plan for developing a healthy journaling lifestyle.

Step 1: Define Your Goals

Your journal should develop organically as a reflection of your spiritual formation goals and needs, so begin by deciding what you want to get out of journaling.

I want to keep a journal so that...

My three main goals for keeping a journal are...

1)

2)

3)

My hope is that keeping a journal will facilitate the development of the following spiritual disciplines (consider reviewing the lists of disciplines in Chapters 3, 6, and 7):

Step 2: Select Your Journal

Refer to Chapter 3 for guidance.

Select your preference for each of the following:

Method: _____ Digital _____ Print

Size: _____ Small _____ Standard

Inside: _____ Lined _____ Unlined

Cost-related:

_____ Inexpensive notebook

_____ Artist sketchbook

_____ Something that fits my personality

_____ Moleskine

Step 3: Organize Your System

Over time, you will develop a system that meets your unique spiritual formation goals and needs for journaling. As you begin, consider the following.

- **Preference.** Will you keep one journal, like I do, or will you keep multiple journals? Both are valid options. Just make sure you can clearly articulate your reasoning why so that you are comfortable with your decision.

  I prefer to keep one or multiple journals because...

- **Content.** List the content that you plan to include in your journal(s) below. To get your creative juices flowing, remember that Richard Peace suggests the following categories: daily, history, dialogue, pilgrimage, Bible study, dreams, musings, family, and work.[11]

  I will write about the following in my journal(s):

Step 4: Make Your Plan

The following prompts guide you in developing a six-week plan to help you establish a habit of journaling.

I would describe my current season of life with its unique limitations and blessings as...

Over the next six weeks, I commit to write in my journal:

_____ *Daily*

_____ *Every other day*

_____ *Twice weekly*

_____ *On Sabbath*

I will write for _____ minutes each time.

In order to make time and space to do this, I will...

Step 5: Plan Your Defense

Remember, journaling regularly can be tough. You can expect that there will always be "something" to convince you not to journal. It takes at least six weeks to establish the habit of journaling, but less than a week to break it. Thus, you need a plan to defend your journaling against talking yourself out of journaling because of "rational" excuses. Proactively, your plan should also involve a close spiritual friend who will regularly ask you about the quality of your journaling.

- **Rational excuses.** "Rational" excuses may include your car breaking down, a large project at work, your child getting sick, or a snowstorm. These are "rational" excuses because you will use them to "rationalize" not writing in your journal.

List the three most likely things that could derail your plan.

1)

2)

3)

When something poses as a "rational" excuse to avoid journaling, I will maintain focus and intentionality and will keep with my plan by doing the following:

- **Spiritual friendship.** Spiritual friends who regularly ask you about the quality (content) of your journaling help you maintain the quantity (amount) of your journaling. Quality-type questions include: "How have you experienced Jesus in your daily life lately?" "What is the Lord teaching you lately?" "When was the last time your heart welled up in worship?" "How is it with your soul?"

  I will ask the following person(s) to share my spiritual journey over the next six weeks by asking me quality questions about my journaling:

Now that you have worked through your journaling plan, you can get started. So, what are you waiting for? Grab your pen (or keyboard) and start writing!

Endnotes

1   Peace, Richard. *Spiritual Journaling: Recording Your Journey Toward God.* Colorado Springs: NavPress, 1998, p. 10. Used by permission of NavPress, All Rights Reserved. www. navpress.com.

2   Taken from *Spiritual Disciplines Handbook: Practices That Transform Us* by Adele Ahlberg Calhoun. Copyright © 2005 by Adele Ahlberg Calhoun. Used by permission of InterVarsity Press, P.O. Box 1400, Downers Grove, IL 60515, USA. www. ivpress.com, p. 57.

3   Peace, *Spiritual Journal*, p. 10.

4   Calhoun, *Spiritual Disciplines Handbook*, p. 56.

5   Calhoun, *Spiritual Disciplines Handbook*, p. 56.

6   Taken from *Invitation to a Journey: A Road Map for Spiritual Formation* by M. Robert Mulholland Jr. Copyright © 1993 by M. Robert Mulholland Jr. Used by permission of InterVarsity Press, P.O. Box 1400, Downers Grove, IL 60515, USA. www.ivpress.com, Kindle Electronic Edition, Locations 40-41.

7   Calhoun, *Spiritual Disciplines Handbook*, p. 57.

8   Peace, *Spiritual Journal*, p98.

9   Mulholland, *Invitation to a Journey*, Kindle Locations 40-41.

10   Mulholland, *Invitation to a Journey*, Kindle Locations 33-39.

11   Peace, *Spiritual Journal*, p. 98.

About the Author

Biography

Rev. Dr. Adam L. Feldman is a pastor, spiritual director, writer, and church planter assessor and coach. He is the founding church planter and current Pastor of Spiritual Formation and Preaching at Metanoia Church in Ellicott City, Maryland. Adam holds a D.Min. in spiritual formation from Gordon-Conwell Theological Seminary, an M.Div. from New Orleans Baptist Theological Seminary, and a B.A. in English (Creative Writing) and Communication Arts from Carson-Newman University. He lives in the Baltimore area with his wife, Kim, and children, Abby and Joshua.

Read more about Adam and invite him to speak at your next engagement, facilitate your next retreat, or write an article for you at http://www.AdamLFeldman.com/allabout/

Connect

Blog

http://www.AdamLFeldman.com

Twitter

@adamlfeldman

Google+

https://plus.google.com/+AdamFeldman/

Facebook

https://www.facebook.com/Feldman.Adam.L

Encouraging the Pilgrim

Equipping the Practitioner

Manufactured by Amazon.ca
Bolton, ON

21462684R00083